SUCCEEDING WITH THE BOOCH AND OMT METHODS:

A PRACTICAL APPROACH

The Addison-Wesley Series
in Object-Oriented Software Engineering

Grady Booch, Series Editor

Grady Booch, *Object Solutions: Managing the Object-Oriented Project*
0-8053-0594-7

Grady Booch, *Object-Oriented Analysis and Design with Applications, Second Edition*
0-8053-5340-2

Grady Booch and Doug Bryan, *Software Engineering with ADA, Third Edition*
0-8053-0608-0

Dave Collins, *Designing Object-Oriented User Interfaces*
0-8053-5350-X

Wilf LaLonde, *Discovering Smalltalk*
0-8053-2720-7

Ira Pohl, *Object-Oriented Programming Using C++*
0-8053-5382-8 (Second Edition available fall 1996)

David N. Smith, *IBM Smalltalk: The Language*
0-8053-0908-X

Daniel Tkach and Richard Puttick, *Object Technology in Application Development, Second Edition*
0-8054-9833-2

Daniel Tkach, Walter Fang, and Andrew So, *Visual Modeling Technique: Object Technology Using Visual Programming*
0-8053-2574-3

Lockheed Martin Advanced Concepts Center and Rational Software Corporation, *Succeeding with the Booch and OMT Methods: A Practical Approach*
0-8053-2279-5

New for Fall 1996

David Bellin and Susan Suchman Simone, *The CRC Card Book*
0-201-89535-8

Martin Fowler, *Analysis Patterns: Reusable Object Models*
0-201-89542-0

Robert Hathaway, *Object-Technology FAQ*
0-201-89541-2

Thomas Mowbray and William Ruh, *Introduction to CORBA*
0-201-89540-4

SUCCEEDING WITH THE BOOCH AND OMT METHODS:

A PRACTICAL APPROACH

LOCKHEED MARTIN
ADVANCED CONCEPTS CENTER

RATIONAL SOFTWARE CORPORATION

 **ADDISON-WESLEY**

An imprint of Addison Wesley Longman, Inc.

Menlo Park, California • Reading, Massachusetts • Harlow, England
Berkeley, California • Don Mills, Ontario • Sydney • Bonn • Amsterdam • Tokyo • Mexico City

Acquisitions Editor: J. Carter Shanklin
Editorial Assistant: Angela Buening
Senior Production Editor: Teri Hyde
Manufacturing Coordinator: Janet Weaver
Text Design & Composition: London Road Design
Composition and Film Buyer: Vivian McDougal

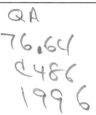

QA
76.64
C486
1996

Many of the designations used by the manufacturers and sellers to distinguish their products are claimed as trademarks. Where those designations appear in this book, and Addison-Wesley was aware of a trademark claim, the designations have been printed in initial caps or all caps.

This document is intended to provide the customer with an introduction to the concepts, terminology, and practical issues related to the use of visual modeling technique in an application development environment.

The information in this document is not intended as a specification of the interfaces that are provided by any of the products mentioned in this publication.

Printed in the United States of America.

Library of Congress Cataloging-in-Publication Data
Quatrani, Terry.
    Succeeding with the Booch and OMT methods : a practical approach /
Terry Quatrani, Michael Chonoles.
        p.   cm.
    Includes index.
    ISBN 0-8053-2279-5
    1. Object-oriented programming (Computer science). 2. Computer software—
Development.   I. Chonoles, Michael. II. Title.
    QA76.64.Q38 1996
    005.1'2—dc20   96-8640
                                                          CIP

ISBN 0-8053-2279-5
1 2 3 4 5 6 7 8 9 10 MA 00 99 98 97 96

Addison-Wesley Publishing Company
2725 Sand Hill Road
Menlo Park, CA 94025

2-4-97

We would like to thank our families, Susann and Zev Chonoles, and Ernie, Mike, Matt, and Steve Quatrani for all their support.

Michael Jesse Chonoles
Terry Quatrani

Contents

Preface

GOALS

THIS BOOK PROVIDES practical guidance on the construction of object-oriented systems using the Booch and OMT methods of software development. Its specific goals are

- To provide a sound understanding of the fundamental principles of the Booch and OMT methods
- To give examples of the usage of the key elements of the notations
- To teach the application of the Booch and OMT methods by using a sample problem domain

AUDIENCE

THIS BOOK IS written for the computer professional as well as for the student. It is suitable for use in professional seminars and individual study as well as in undergraduate and graduate courses. It shows how to

- Use the Booch and OMT methods effectively to solve real problems
- Develop a system from requirements to detailed design by using an object-oriented approach

Because this is a case study, the reader should have a general understanding of or be in the process of learning the approach, the specialized terms, and the notation of the Booch[1] and/or OMT[2] methods. This book also assumes some familiarity with basic software engineering concepts.

APPROACH

THIS BOOK TAKES a practical approach to teaching the Booch and OMT methods. It uses a case study to show the analysis and design of an application. We chose a course registration system for a university as the problem domain because it is easily understood and not specific to any field of computer science. The reader can concentrate on the specifics of modeling the domain in the Booch and OMT methods, rather than investing time in understanding an unfamiliar problem domain.

The problem is treated seriously enough to give the reader practical experience with most of the steps of the Booch and OMT methods and the feeling of solving a real problem, without being so realistic that the reader is bogged down in details. Thus many interesting and perhaps necessary requirements, considerations, and constraints were put aside to produce a simplified, yet useful case study fitting the scope of this book. With the goal of usefulness in mind, the exercises have been crafted to make the methods clear to a practitioner's eye.

The methods are described as a series of sequential steps. This approach gives the new user a framework for developing object-oriented applications and provides advanced techniques for more experienced users. As users become fluent in the methods, they will be able to move back and forth through the steps, and often combine several steps, until the desired result is achieved.

For additional details on the evolving Booch and OMT methods, or on applying them to your application, you should consider the training and mentoring services offered by both the Lockheed

---

[1] Booch, Grady, *Object-Oriented Analysis and Design with Applications.* Redwood City, Calif.: Benjamin/Cummings, 1993.

[2] Rumbaugh, James, et al., *Object-Oriented Modeling and Design.* Englewood Cliffs, N.J.: Prentice Hall, 1991.

Martin Advanced Concepts Center (ACC) and Rational Software Corporation. The ACC may be contacted at Lockheed Martin Advanced Concepts Center, 640 Freedom Business Center, King of Prussia, PA 19406, 1-800-438-7246. You may send e-mail to the ACC at solutions@acc.vf.mmc.com. Rational Software Corporation may be contacted at 2800 San Tomas Expressway, Santa Clara, CA 95051, 1-800-767-3237. You may send e-mail to Rational at product_info@rational.com.

Any software development method is best supported by a tool, and this book makes use of the tool Rational Rose 3.0. Each step in either method includes a description of how to use Rational Rose 3.0 to complete the step. This information is presented in separate text boxes provided as an aid to users of Rational Rose 3.0. To obtain a copy of Rational Rose 3.0, contact either of the above companies.

STRUCTURE

THE BOOK IS divided into three sections followed by a set of appendices. The first section contains case-study background information that is applicable to both the Booch and OMT methods. The second section contains chapters devoted to the Booch method, and the third section covers the OMT method.

CASE-STUDY BACKGROUND

THE FIRST CHAPTER discusses information related to the course registration system case study that is used throughout the book.

THE BOOCH METHOD

Overview

Chapter 2 establishes the principles of the Booch method. It summarizes the steps of the method, and discusses the deliverables of each step.

Conceptualization

Chapter 3 discusses possible sources of information about the requirements of a system and shows the creation of a context diagram. It also describes the problem domain of the course registration system used throughout the book.

Analysis

Chapters 4 through 9 describe the steps of analysis in detail. Chapter 4 discusses how to find, define, and document key classes of the domain. Chapter 5 shows how to define the structure and behavior of the system by looking at the use cases of the system. Chapter 6 illustrates the definition of relationships between classes in the system. Chapter 7 discusses the discovery of generalized classes, or superclasses, and of specialized classes, or subclasses. Chapter 8 illustrates the use of Harel state transition diagrams for classes with significant dynamic behavior. Finally, Chapter 9 presents ways to validate an analysis model.

Design

Chapters 10 through 12 describe how an analysis model matures into a design model. Chapter 10 shows how to organize the design into a structured architecture. Chapter 11 details the steps involved in iteration planning. Chapter 12 discusses the use of commercial class libraries during development.

Evolution

Chapters 13 through 15 describe the evolution of a system under development using an iterative and incremental approach. Chapter 13 discusses building an iteration. Chapter 14 illustrates the steps necessary to build the next iteration. Finally, Chapter 15 details team development procedures.

THE OMT METHOD

Overview

Chapter 16 establishes the principles of the OMT method. It summarizes the steps of the method, the models, and the deliverables of each step.

Conceptualization

Chapter 17 explains how OMT can help you understand the need for a system and to systematically obtain the outline and form of new systems. Showing how to create context diagrams and high-level use cases, this chapter introduces the problem domain of the course registration system and the operation concepts of the solution approach used throughout the book.

Domain Analysis

Domain analysis, the systematic exploration of the world, is examined in Chapters 18 through 21. The core modeling approaches of OMT, the class diagram (Chapter 18), associations (Chapter 19), operations and attributes (Chapter 20), and state diagrams (Chapter 21), are also covered.

Application Analysis

In Chapters 22 through 25, we further analyze the specific application. Application classes (Chapter 22), such as surrogates, controllers, and views are created, and use cases (Chapter 23) are further explored to capture the specific user-visible requirements of the system. Chapter 24 discusses the discovery of generalized classes, or superclasses, and of specialized classes, or subclasses. In Chapter 25, the functional model is introduced to formally capture lower-level behavior. Chapter 26 discusses techniques to test the analysis.

System Design

System architecture and policy are captured using techniques described in Chapter 27.

Object Design

The details of object design are captured using diagrams such as the object interaction diagrams, as shown in Chapter 28. Chapter 29 discusses the use of commercial class libraries during development. As object design progresses, the details of the objects are specified. Chapter 30 gives an overview of some of the considerations of object design and begins to discuss implementation.

Implementation

After the discussion in Chapter 30 of implementation, Chapter 31 illustrates the steps necessary to build the next iteration using round-trip engineering. Finally, Chapter 32 details team development procedures.

Appendix A

Appendix A gives a detailed definition of the Booch notation.

Appendix B

Appendix B gives a detailed definition of the OMT notation.

Appendix C

Appendix C shows a sample of the C++ code generated by the Rational Rose 3.0 tool for one class in the course registration system.

USING THIS BOOK

YOU CAN READ straight through this manual to obtain the fundamental concepts of the Booch and OMT methods and a sense of how the object-oriented software engineering process works. Using the book along with Rational Rose 3.0 will allow you to work some of the examples and develop a more detailed understanding of the methods.

ACKNOWLEDGMENTS

WE WOULD LIKE to thank the following people for their contributions to the content, style, presentation, and writing of this book. Special thanks to Loren Archer, Alex Baran, Grady Booch, Elizabeth Bufo, Mike Duffy, Frank DuPont, Jim Ford, Adam Frankel, Burton Goldfield, Kim Heisman, Peter Luckey, Phil Magrogan, Sue Mickel, Paul Mims, Sylvia Pacheco, Jim Rumbaugh, Jim Schardt, Tom Schultz, Bill Snizek, Mark Sutton, Kurt TeKolste, Chuck von Flotow, and Daryl Winters for all their inputs.

Chapter 1

Case Study Background

THE IMPORTANCE OF PROPER CONCEPTUALIZATION

THE MOST IMPORTANT question to ask when developing a system is neither a methodological nor a technical question. It is a most simple question: "Is this the right system to make?" Unfortunately, this question is often neither asked nor answered. Although misguided methodology or technically tough problems may cause projects to fail, sufficient resources and heroic effort by talented people can often save them—but nothing can save a system that is not needed or that automates the wrong thing.

Conceptualization is the phase that asks the appropriate questions and gathers the right information to answer that tough question. It determines the system to be built and its high-level outline and structure, based on business needs and available technology.

Before starting a project, we must have an idea for it. Conceptualization is the process of coming up with an idea for a system along with a general idea of its requirements and form. It finishes the statement, "The system we want is . . . " An adequate conceptualization establishes the high-level requirements for a desirable and feasible system, both technologically and sociologically. Inadequate conceptualizations lead to systems so unwanted, expensive, impossible, and ill-defined that they are typically not finished or used.

THE CONCEPTUALIZATION PROCESS

CONCEPTUALIZATION CAN BE done formally or informally, but it always involves considering the business needs, the available resources, the possible technology, and the desires of the user community, along with several ideas for new systems. Brainstorming, research, trade studies, cost-benefit analyses, use-case analysis, and prototyping can then be performed to produce the target system's concept along with defined purposes, priorities, and context. Usually, preliminary resource and schedule planning are also done during the conceptualization phase.

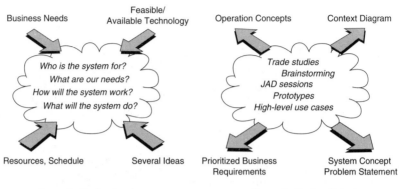

Business Needs   Feasible/ Available Technology   Operation Concepts   Context Diagram

Who is the system for?
What are our needs?
How will the system work?
What will the system do?

Trade studies
Brainstorming
JAD sessions
Prototypes
High-level use cases

Resources, Schedule   Several Ideas   Prioritized Business Requirements   System Concept Problem Statement

Conceptualization Inputs   **Conceptualization Outputs**

For some projects, a conceptualization can be sketched on the back of a napkin. For others, conceptualization may be a formal phase that is iteratively performed until enough levels of detail have been specified for the target system. However it is done, any conceptualization requires some amount of analysis and design. Analysis activity during conceptualization is performed to capture the understanding of the domain and current systems needs, and design activity is performed when the new system outlines and architecture are chosen.

CASE STUDY BACKGROUND

THE FOLLOWING SAMPLE problem, the ESU course registration system, will be used throughout this book to illustrate the steps and procedures of the Booch and OMT methods.

The process of assigning professors to courses and the registration of students is a frustrating and time-consuming experience. The students currently fill out (mulitpart, multicolor) registration forms that indicate their choice of courses and return the completed forms to the Registrar's Office. The typical student load is four courses. The staff of the Registrar's Office then enters the data from each of the student's forms into the mainframe computer system. Once that is done, a batch job is run overnight to assign students to courses. Students usually get their first choices; however, when there is a conflict, the Registrar's Office asks each student for additional

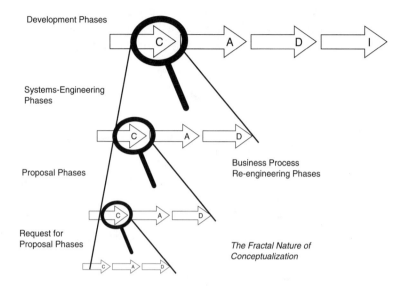

Development Phases

Systems-Engineering
Phases

Proposal Phases

Request for
Proposal Phases

Business Process
Re-engineering Phases

*The Fractal Nature of
Conceptualization*

choices. When all the students have been successfully assigned to courses, they receive hard copies of their curricula for verification. Most student registrations are processed within a week, but some exceptional cases take up to two weeks to solve.

After the professors at ESU have decided which courses they are going to teach for the semester, the Registrar's Office enters the information into the computer system. A batch report is printed for the professors indicating which courses they will teach and the student roster for each course. The fact that students must pick courses before the professors have been assigned to teach them has been a constant source of confusion and frustration to the students.

BUSINESS GOALS AND NEEDS

THE FIRST QUESTION to ask is whether the university really needs a new registration system, and if so, how important it is. Though the current registration system doesn't sound that good, there are competing demands for the resources. The Bursar's Office, for example, could also use overhauling. The goals of the business or enterprise must be understood to evaluate the severity of the problem. Then the available resources can be allocated properly among all possible ventures. Understanding the business goals allows the organization as a whole and the development team to accomplish the following:

- Determine which existing system most needs overhauling
- Decide whether an existing system meets business goals sufficiently
- Allocate resources among the several competing potential ventures
- Outline the changes to a system that will provide the most cost-effective results
- Check proposed requirements against business needs
- Make consistent optimizing decisions during design

Many organizations have an internally published vision or mission statement that is a good resource for understanding the organization's business goals. Otherwise, it may be necessary to work closely with the key representatives of the business to determine their priorities and goals, and perhaps to hold facilitated sessions of the key stakeholders. Business requirements often specify such goals as increased market share, improved time-to-market, improved customer satisfaction, improved quality, decreased failure rate, decreased service time, decreased price, and increased availability.

Representatives of the key university stakeholders should be involved to determine the relevant business goals. Each university will have different groups, including the following:

- University Administration
- Registrar's Office
- Professors
- Students
- Campus Computer and Network Administration
- Campus Safety/Security
- Development Organization

- Union or Staff Representatives
- Public Relations
- Quality of Campus Life Committees

Some of the relevant business goals of the university are as follows:

- The students' and professors' interactions with the university should be quick, simple, and satisfactory
- Minimize nonacademic administrative staff positions
- Shorten presemester preparation and registration time
- Decrease seasonal fluctuations in required staff
- Reduce peak pedestrian and vehicle traffic during registration
- Utilize existing computer and system resources
- System must be fully available by the start of the next semester

RISKS FOR THE COURSE REGISTRATION PROBLEM

THE DEVELOPMENT TEAM identified the major risk to the system as the ability to efficiently store and access the curriculum information. They developed several prototypes that evaluated data storage and access mechanisms for each database management system under consideration. The results of the prototypes led to the decision to use a particular relational database management system. Additional prototypes were also developed to study the hardware required for the university to move to a paperless registration system.

SUMMARY

CONCEPTUALIZATION IS AN iterative approach that produces the inputs for object-oriented analysis. Customers, clients, users, and other stakeholders bring good ideas to conceptualization and offer the possibility of early and enthusiastic buy-in.

GLOSSARY

BACKGROUND PROBLEM STATEMENT

Cumulative background material assembled before working on a project. It often includes a description and critique of the previous system.

BUSINESS GOALS

Prioritized statements of the organization's needs used to guide decision making and trade-off throughout the development process.

STAKEHOLDERS

The stakeholders of a system are the people and organizations that have a stake in the operation of the system. They can include such diverse groups as management, employees, shareholders, subcontractors, operators, users, regulatory and standards groups, consumers, and affected neighbors.

Chapter 2

Overview of the Booch Method

THE BOOCH METHOD

THE BOOCH METHOD is an object-oriented software development method used to analyze, model, and document system requirements. It was developed by Grady Booch, based on more than fifteen years of practical development experience with large, complex applications. "The Booch notation is both usable and well known. Of all the notations I have seen, it contains the most expressive power, because it contains the largest repertoire of icons and symbols for the expression of relationships, objects, class types, and their modifiers."[1]

The Booch method is classified as a second-generation, object-oriented analysis and design method. It unifies his earlier work with concepts from Objectory, OMT, and other methods, as shown in the figure on page 12.

Use cases and interaction diagrams were adopted from the Objectory methodology. Analysis concepts such as associations, keys, constraints, and attributed associations were incorporated from the OMT methodology. CRC (class, responsibility, collaboration) cards were added to facilitate brainstorming activities. Responsibility-driven design methods added the concepts of roles and responsibilities. Hierarchical state machines come from Harel. Formalism added the need to precisely specify the syntax and semantics of the Booch notation. From the patterns movement, Booch has incorporated the notion of a pattern itself as well as the concept of a note. The method has adopted metrics from the work of Chidamber and Kemerer, of the MIT Sloan School of Management. Finally, experience with the SEI process maturity models and the emerging requirements of standards such as ISO 9000 added to the definition of the Booch process. Clearly, "The Booch method is a major step in the direction of convergence and thus represents a waging of peace in the method wars."[2]

---

[1] Martin, Robert C. *Designing Object-Oriented C++ Applications Using the Booch Method,* Englewood Cliffs, N.J.: Prentice Hall, 1995.

[2] Booch, Grady. "The Evolution of the Booch Method." *ROAD* 1(1), 1994.

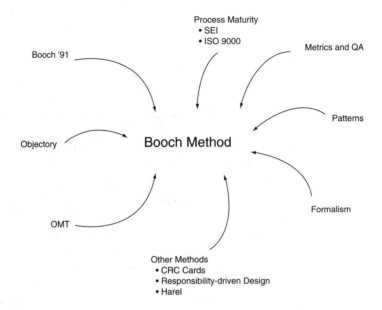

WHY PROCESS IS NEEDED

A SUCCESSFUL DEVELOPMENT project satisfies or exceeds the customer's expectations, is developed in a timely and economical fashion, and is resilient to change and adaptation. The development life cycle must promote creativity and innovation. At the same time, the development process must be controlled and measured to ensure that the project is indeed completed." Creativity is essential to the crafting of all well-structured object-oriented architectures, but developers allowed completely unrestrained creativity tend to never reach closure. Similarly, discipline is required when organizing the efforts of a team of developers, but too much discipline gives birth to an ugly bureaucracy that kills all attempts at innovation."[3] A well-managed iterative and incremental life cycle provides the necessary control without affecting creativity.

---

[3] Booch, Grady. *Object Solutions.* Redwood City, Calif.: Addison-Wesley, 1995.

THE ROLE OF NOTATION

NOTATION PLAYS AN important part in any methodology—it is the glue that holds the process together. The Booch method provides a very robust notation, which grows from analysis into design. Certain elements of the notation (i.e., classes, association, aggregations, inheritance) are introduced during analysis. Other elements of the notation (i.e., class categories, containment indicators, and adornments) are introduced during design and evolution.

"Notation has three roles:

- It serves as the language for communicating decisions that are not obvious or cannot be inferred from the code itself.

- It provides semantics that are rich enough to capture all important strategic and tactical decisions.

- It offers a form concrete enough for humans to reason about and for tools to manipulate."[4]

ITERATIVE AND INCREMENTAL LIFE CYCLE

IN AN ITERATIVE and incremental life cycle, development proceeds as a series of architectural releases that evolve into the final system. The developers do not assume that all requirements are known at the beginning of the life cycle; indeed, change is anticipated throughout all phases. It is a risk-mitigation-driven process.

Technical risks are assessed and prioritized early in the life cycle and are reviewed during the development of each architectural release. Risks are attached to each iteration so that its successful completion would mitigate the attached risks. The releases are scheduled to ensure that the highest risks are tackled first. Building the system in this fashion exposes and mitigates the risks of the system early in the life cycle, and integration of the "pieces" of the system is continual. The result of this type of life cycle is less risk coupled with minimal investment.

---

[4] Ibid.

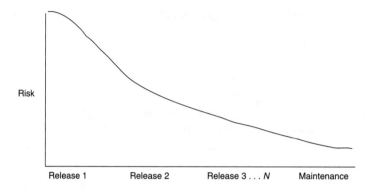

Control for an iterative and incremental life cycle is described by Booch using a macro and micro process.

THE MACRO PROCESS

THE MACRO PROCESS is a high-level process describing the activities of the development team as a whole. It approaches the development process from a manager's perspective. The macro process consists of the steps, or phases, shown in the figure below.

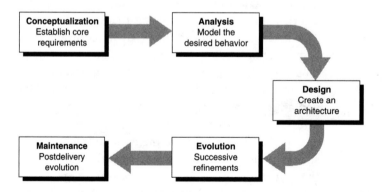

During conceptualization a vision for the idea is established, and many assumptions are either validated or rejected. The activities that occur involve the solicitation of ideas, the prioritization of tasks to be accomplished, and possibly some "proof-of-concept" prototypes. In addition, a context diagram showing the system under consideration along with its external interfaces is developed. The primary output from this phase is a set of core requirements for the system. "For projects of modest complexity whose full life cycle is about one year, the conceptualization phase typically lasts about one month."[5]

Analysis is the process of capturing and understanding the complete and consistent set of system requirements. It is the "what" of the problem, *not* the "how" of the problem. Use cases are developed for each of the major external actors identified in the context diagram. For each use case, scenarios are developed and shown graphically in object message diagrams and/or message trace diagrams. Objects and classes are discovered in the scenarios and shown in the initial class diagram. The structure and behavior of the objects are added to the class diagram. All work done during analysis is from the user point of view as opposed to a developer point of view. "For projects of modest complexity whose full life cycle is about one year, the analysis phase typically lasts about one to two months."[6]

The design phase might more aptly be titled the architectural phase, because its focus is on the construction of the software architecture, both logical and physical. The software architecture is constructed by identifying horizontal layers with well-defined purposes and interfaces that build on top of each other. The logical layers are built out of class categories. A mapping is made from class categories to subsystems, so that the physical layers are made out of subsystems. One of the major activities during the design phase is release planning. During the analysis phase the technical risks of the system were assessed and prioritized. Now the risks must be attached to releases to ensure that the successful completion of the release will mitigate the risks. Attaching, or assigning, risks to releases is accomplished by first slicing out partitions from the layered architecture. The contents and boundaries of the partitions are determined by grouping together closely related use cases that define major system functions. Risks are assigned to partitions so that implementing a partition will mitigate the risks. Partitions are assigned to releases so that the highest risks are handled first. "For projects of modest complexity whose full life cycle is about one

---

[5] Ibid.

[6] Ibid.

year, the design phase typically lasts about one month and rarely exceeds two months."[7]

The next step of the process is evolution. During this phase the system is matured by implementing a succession of executable releases. Each release is an increment of the system, defined by one or more partitions, and adds to the functionality provided by all previous releases. Development continues by applying the micro process to each architectural release. "For projects of modest complexity whose full life cycle is about one year, the evolution phase typically lasts about nine months."[8]

The last step of the macro process is maintenance. The main activity of this phase is managing the post delivery evolution of the system, which includes plans for future releases of the system.

THE MICRO PROCESS

THE MICRO PROCESS is a lower-level process that represents the technical activities of the development team. It is composed of the steps shown in the figure below.

This process is applied to each architectural release of the system.

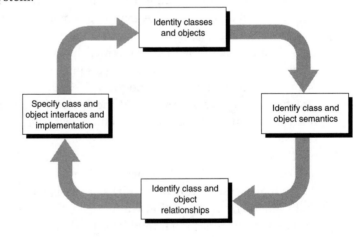

---

[7] Ibid.

[8] Ibid.

The first step is to identify classes and objects. Here, the concentration is on the particular release being developed. Classes to be developed during the current release are identified and documented.

Next, classes and object semantics are refined. Additional scenario diagrams may be produced that allow the designer to fully investigate object structure and behavior for the release. Object structure and behavior are captured as attributes and operations in the class. Documentation is updated to include the additional information discovered during this phase.

Class and object relationships are designed during the next phase. Associations may be refined into "has" relationships or "uses" relationships. The class diagram is updated to reflect the relationship designs. Scenario diagrams and the class diagram are compared to verify communication between objects. Cardinality estimates made during analysis are refined at this stage of the process.

The last step is to specify class and object interfaces and implementations. Data types for attributes and signatures for operations are added to each class. An algorithm is selected for each operation, and helper operations are added to the classes. During each step of the micro process, existing classes may be modified or new classes may be added to mature the design of the architectural release.

DISCOVERY, INVENTION, AND IMPLEMENTATION

EVERY SUCCESSFUL PROJECT contains cycles of discovery, invention, and implementation that provide the focus for the analysts and designers during the different phases of the macro and micro processes. These cycles are shown in the following figure on page 18.[9]

Discovery provides an understanding of the required system behavior. This activity peaks during analysis, but never completely goes away. Invention leads to the creation of a system's architecture; it peaks during design when the major strategic and tactical decisions are made. Invention can start early in the life cycle with the development of prototypes and continues during evolution.

Implementation involves coding, testing, and integration. It peaks during evolution, as the decisions made during design are carried out.

---

[9] Kruchten, Philippe. *Software Architecture and Iterative Process.* Santa Clara, Calif.: Rational Software Corporation, 1994.

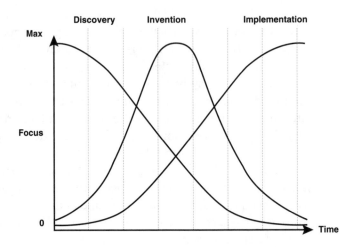

SETTING UP RATIONAL ROSE FOR BOOCH

1. Choose Default Notation from the Options menu.
2. Choose Booch.

The Rational Rose class diagram editor with Booch notation is shown below.

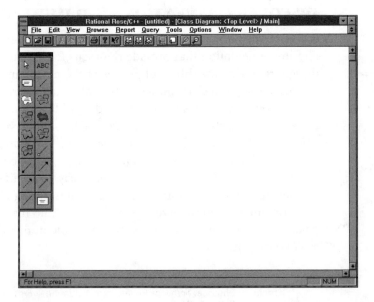

SUMMARY

COMBINING THE MACRO and the micro processes to complete an iterative and incremental life cycle can be illustrated using a "little b" model. The micro process is applied multiple times during the evolution phase, and in some form, it can also be applied during the other three phases.

Object-oriented analysis, design, and programming used in conjunction with an iterative and incremental process is a means of providing a good, sound software engineering process for analysts, designers, and programmers. It begins with a model of requirements from a user point of view. The model is matured during design as the focus shifts from a user point of view to a developer point of view. Code for the model is developed for each architectural release of the system.

Summary

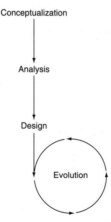

GLOSSARY

ANALYSIS

> The process of capturing and understanding the complete and consistent set of system requirements.

CONCEPTUALIZATION
> Phase of development where a vision for the idea is established and assumptions are validated.

DESIGN
> Phase of development where an architecture for the implementation is created and tactical policies are established.

DISCOVERY
> Phase of development that leads to an understanding of a system's required behavior.

EVOLUTION
> Phase of development where the implementation is matured through a succession of executable releases.

IMPLEMENTATION
> Phase of development where the major focus is the development of a deliverable application.

INVENTION
> Phase of development where the major focus is the creation of a system's architecture.

ITERATIVE AND INCREMENTAL LIFE CYCLE
> Development of a series of architectural releases that evolve into the final system.

MACRO PROCESS
> High-level process describing the activities of the development team as a whole.

MAINTENANCE
> Management of the post delivery evolution of the system.

MICRO PROCESS
> Lower-level process that represents the technical activities of the development team.

Chapter 3

Conceptualization: Defining the Problem

DEFINING THE PROBLEM

CONCEPTUALIZATION ESTABLISHES A vision for the idea, and validates
or rejects many assumptions. The activities that occur involve the
solicitation of ideas, the preliminary identification of risks, and possibly some "proof-of-concept" prototypes. Ideas come from many
sources: customers, domain experts, other developers, industry
experts, feasibility studies, and/or review of existing systems. Any
prototyping done during this phase should be considered throw-
away code, because the code is generated merely to support a list of
assumptions; it has not been fully analyzed or designed. A context
diagram showing the system under consideration along with its
external interfaces is also developed. The primary output from this
phase is a set of core requirements for the system.

IDENTIFYING THE ACTORS

USE-CASE ANALYSIS often starts during conceptualization. Here the
actors that interact with the system are identified. An actor is a role
played by a physical person or object when interfacing with the system. These actors are usually discovered in the problem statement,
in conversations with customers and domain experts, or by examining the outputs from previous levels of conceptualization.

For the ESU course registration problem, the following external
actors have been identified: Student, Professor, Administrator, and
the Billing System. The same individual may act in more than one
role at different times, such as a professor who also takes courses,
but the responsibilities of each role are different.

DRAWING A CONTEXT DIAGRAM

ONE OF THE first steps for any system development effort is defining
the scope of the problem. A context diagram is a graphical way of
showing the boundaries of a system along with inputs and outputs

to the system. A context diagram is a high-level object message diagram. The system and all external actors are shown as objects. Inputs and outputs are shown as "messages" to and from the object representing the system.

The external actors are often discussed in the problem statement. Conversations with customers and domain experts also lead to the discovery of external actors. Each role that a physical person plays while interacting with the system becomes a different external actor, although an external actor does not have to be a physical person—another system may also be an external actor to the system under consideration.

CREATING CONTEXT DIAGRAMS IN RATIONAL ROSE

1. Choose Scenario Diagram from the Browse menu option.
2. Double-click on < New > to display the New Scenario window.
3. Type Context Diagram in the Title field of the New Scenario window.
4. Select the Object Message radio button.
5. Click the OK button.

The New Scenario window is shown below.

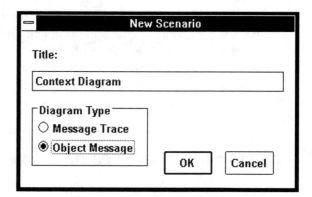

CREATING THE SYSTEM OBJECT AND
ACTOR OBJECTS IN RATIONAL ROSE

1. Select the object icon (solid cloud) from the tool palette.
2. Click on the diagram window.
3. Type the name of the system in the cloud.
4. Repeat the steps above for each actor.
5. Select the link icon (line) from the tool palette, click on the object representing the system, and drag the link to an object representing an actor.
6. Repeat step 5 for each actor.
7. To create inputs to and outputs from the system, select the message icon (arrow), and click on the link between the actor and the system.
8. Type the name of the inputs and outputs on the message arrows.

For the ESU course registration problem, the following external actors have been identified by examining the problem statement: Student, Professor, Administrator, and Billing System. The context diagram for the ESU course registration problem follows on page 26.

OPERATIONS CONCEPTS

TO CONTINUE DEVELOPING such a system any further, you need more of an idea of how it will work. For example, the context diagram could be true of the existing paper/mainframe system as well as many possible, more automated systems. Though it is important to keep the possibilities open, you also need to get a picture, a *concept*, of how the system will work.

The operations concepts capture a description of how the system will be used, to distinguish it from other potential system solutions. They often contain a description of the target market—the subsets of actors that would want to (or could) use the system and the prerequisite hardware and software. The focus should be on particular system configurations, so that a picture or vision of the new system will emerge.

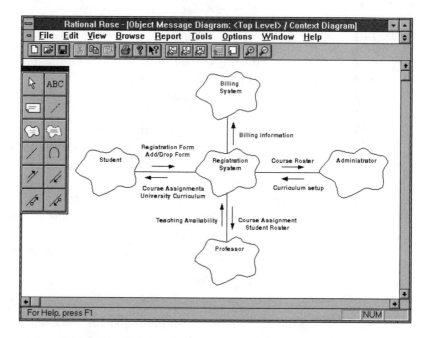

Besides the general system's operations concepts, a general description of the approach and the frequency of each use case or fundamental communication are also needed.

Several operations concepts alternatives are chosen and evaluated by techniques such as brainstorming, facilitated discussions, research, and proof-of-concept prototyping. Each potential solution's costs are then compared to how well they meet the business requirements. This helps to determine the approaches to use in the system.

For example, the Student Registration use case can be done by paper forms, as it is typically done now, but there are other possibilities. Before progress can go much further, we need to know the essential outlines of this use case, that is, whether it will be done by paper forms, special punch cards, hard-wired terminals, dial-up computers, or a phone/keypad interface and IVR (interactive voice response).[1] Similarly, the Student's fundamental communication of

---

[1] For example, the 40,000 students at the University of Quebec at Montreal use their phones to complete their registration process. See "University Uses Off-the Shelf CT-Resources to Upgrade Homegown Automated Student Registration." *Computer TELEPHONY*, June 1995.

identity, currently sent by a combination social security number and handwritten signature, may be sent by user ID and password, or by swiping a student ID card through a magnetic card reader attached to a terminal. It is not necessary to pick only one operations concept; most systems require several ways of accomplishing the same task, at least for backup contingency reasons. Some potential approaches should be scheduled for future releases.

Bounds and ranges on the frequency and performance requirements for the use cases and the fundamental communications must also be determined. At this time we just want to understand the order of magnitude of the requirements. For example, will only one student be able to register at a given time, or will many students be able to use the system simultaneously? How many students should the system be sized for, concurrently and in total—hundreds or thousands? Do we need to size the system for just this university, or do we plan to market the finished system to other universities? In the latter case we should be sure that our system can handle the largest of universities (approximately 50,000 students).

PROBLEM STATEMENT

AFTER THE OPERATIONS concepts for each use case and fundamental communication are determined, they are summarized into a concise, consistent statement of the system that must be built. Incorporating any additional domain information that is available, this problem statement is usually written in narrative paragraph form. In some situations, numbered requirements may be necessary to augment the narrative.

ESU COURSE REGISTRATION PROBLEM STATEMENT

AT THE BEGINNING of each semester, the ESU Registrar's Office will provide a list of courses to students through a new on-line registration system. Information about each course, such as professor, department, and prerequisites will be included to help students make informed decisions.

The new system will allow students to review available courses and select four of them for the coming semester. In addition, each student will indicate two alternative choices in case a course becomes filled or canceled. No course will have more than ten students. No course will have fewer than three students. A course with fewer than three students will be canceled. If there is enough interest in a course, then a second section will be established.

Professors must be able to access the on-line system to indicate which courses they will be teaching. They will also need to see which students have signed up for their courses.

The registration process will last for three days. The first day will be freshman orientation and registration. All other students will arrive on the second day of the semester to register. The third day will be used to resolve any outstanding course assignment conflicts.

Once the course registration process is completed for a student, the registration system sends information to the billing system, so the student can be billed for the semester.

As a semester progresses, students must be able to access the on-line system to add or drop courses.

The university prides itself on academic achievement in the Humanities. Most of the professors, administrators, and students are computer illiterate. Thus this system, unlike the old one, must be easy to use for all concerned.

SUMMARY

THE CONCEPTUALIZATION PHASE is a discovery phase. The problem to be solved is verbalized and discussed among the team and with customers. A context diagram is drawn to show the boundaries of the system. Assumptions are expressed and may be verified or rejected using proof-of-concept prototyping techniques. The output of this phase is a set of core requirements.

GLOSSARY

CONTEXT DIAGRAM

> Graphical way to illustrate the boundaries of a system along with inputs and outputs to and from the system.

EXTERNAL ACTOR

> Someone or something interacting with the system under consideration.

OPERATIONS CONCEPT

> A vision of how a use case, communication, or other feature of a system will work when the system is developed.

PROOF-OF-CONCEPT PROTOTYPE

> Prototype used to validate the initial assumptions stated for a given problem space.

Chapter 4

Analysis: Finding Classes

USE CASES AND SCENARIOS

USE-CASE ANALYSIS was first popularized by Ivar Jacobson, who defined a use case as "a particular form or pattern or exemplar of usage, a scenario that begins with some user of the system initiating some transaction or sequence of interrelated events."[1] The collection of use cases describes the system functions of the application. Use cases are identified by examining requirements documents, drawing on personal expertise, and through interaction with customers, domain experts, and software-testing personnel. The best place to start is to examine each actor identified in the context diagram.

For the course registration problem, the following use cases can be identified for each actor:

Student:	Request curriculum list
	Register for courses
	Drop a course
	Add a course
Administrator:	Set up curriculum
	Add another section to a course
	Cancel a course
	Add a student
	Delete a student
	Add a professor
	Delete a professor
Professor:	Indicate courses to be taught
	Request student list
Billing:	Compute student billing information

The identified use cases provide an initial description of a system's behavior. The use cases are typically at a high level and contain a sequence of events necessary to carry out a particular "use" of the system. Scenarios are then developed for each use case; each

---

[1] Jacobson, Ivar. *Object-Oriented Software Engineering.* Reading, Mass.: Addison-Wesley, 1992.

one yields a primary scenario (the "happy-day" case—all works perfectly) and secondary scenarios (exceptions or variations from the primary scenario). Scenarios document decisions about requirements and provide an excellent communication medium for discussion of the system requirements with customers. "Scenarios speak the language of the end user and the domain expert, and therefore provide a format in which they can state their expectations about the desired behavior of a system to its developers."[2]

The Register for Courses use case yields several scenarios:

1. Four courses are open, and two alternates are not needed.

2. Four courses are not open, and one or both of the alternates are needed.

3. Two courses are not open, and neither alternate is open.

4. Student does not have the proper prerequisites for a course.

Scenario 1: Four courses are open, and two alternates are not needed.

> Student opens registration form.
> Student selects English Lit 101.
> Student selects Humanities 103.
> Student selects World History 107.
> Student selects Greek Philosophy 105.
> Student selects Modern Grammar 111 as an alternate.
> Student selects Middle English Lit 145 as an alternate.
> Student submits the form.
> Registrar checks prerequisites for class 101.
> Registrar checks availability of a seat in class 101 current open section.
> Seat is available.
> Registrar assigns student to class 101.
> Registrar checks availability of classes 103, 107, and 105 current open sections.
> All are available.
> Registrar assigns student to classes 103, 107, and 105.
> Registrar creates the student roster.

---

[2] Booch, Grady. *Object Solutions.* Redwood City, Calif.: Addison-Wesley, 1995.

Scenario 4: Student does not have the proper prerequisites for a course.

> Student selects English Lit 201.
> Student fills out the registration form.
> Student submits the form.
> Registrar checks prerequisites for class 201.
> Class 101 is required.
> Registrar checks student records to see if class 101 was taken.
> Student did not take class 101.
> Registrar notifies student that proper prerequisites were not taken.

The collection, or web, of identified scenarios provides a means of capturing the behavior of the system under development. The scenarios are the starting point for the identification of classes and objects in the system.

There are numerous scenarios for any given system. At this early stage of analysis, it is safe to say that looking at the primary scenarios for each identified actor is enough. When you find that each new scenario repeats many steps from previously identified scenarios, then you have reached the finish line. "This phase of analysis should be drawn to a close once the team has elaborated approximately 80% of a system's primary scenarios along with a representative selection of the secondary ones. Elaborate upon any more, and your analysis will likely reach diminishing returns; elaborate upon any fewer, and you won't have a sufficient understanding of the desired behavior of the system to properly understand the risks."[3]

SCENARIOS AND CLASSES

A CLASS IS a collection of objects with the same structure and behavior. We examine each noun contained in the primary scenarios developed for the system to see if it is a candidate class, remembering that some nouns may be grouped together to form candidate classes. Some nouns may be attributes of classes, some may be outside the

---

[3] Ibid.

problem scope, some may be just language expressions, and some are redundant.

The following nouns appear in the two scenarios described above: student, English Lit 101, section, Humanities 103, World History 107, Greek Philosophy 105, Modern Grammar 111, alternate, Middle English Lit 145, registration form, form, registrar, prerequisites, class 101, class 103, class 107, class 105, assignments, English Lit 201, class 201, student record, and student roster. Based on domain knowledge and interaction with the customer, the following classes were identified for the registration problem: Student, Course, Section, RegistrationForm, Registrar, StudentRoster, and StudentRecord.

As classes are identified, they are entered into a class diagram. A definition is required for each candidate class. The definition should describe what the class does, *not* the structure of the class. It is especially useful to document the roles and responsibilities for each class.

The classes and their definitions for the course registration problem are listed below:

> Student—a person registered to take courses at ESU
> Course—a class offered by the university
> Section—an offering of a course
> RegistrationForm—form containing student choices for registration including student name, student ID, semester, four primary courses, and two alternate courses
> Registrar—the person coordinating the registration process
> StudentRecord—history of all courses taken by a given student
> StudentRoster—a list of course assignments for a given semester

Each project should adopt a set of naming standards for classes to ensure consistency across the project. Standards also lead to more maintainable models and code. This book uses singular nouns with an initial capital letter, no underscores, and no space between words as the standard. It is important to enforce the chosen standards from the beginning of the project.

DEFINING CLASSES IN RATIONAL ROSE

1. Choose New from the File menu option to create a new class diagram.
2. Select the class icon (dotted cloud) from the tool palette.
3. Click on the class diagram to draw the cloud.
4. Type the name of the class inside the cloud.

The classes found in the above scenario are shown in the following class diagram.

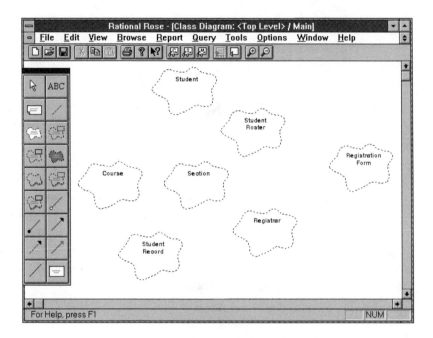

INITIAL CLASS DIAGRAM

THE PROCESS OF developing scenarios and finding candidate classes continues until all the primary use cases described above are complete. The completed initial class diagram is shown on page 38.

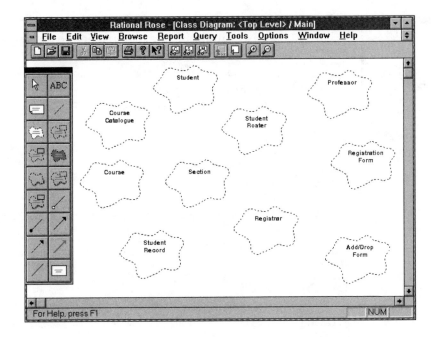

NOTES

MOST SYSTEMS UNDER development include a collection of assumptions and decisions that require documentation. This information is contained in a note, which may be attached to any of the elements in the model. In the course registration problem, the Registrar class is the controller for the system, and this information is documented in a note attached to the class.

DEFINING NOTES IN RATIONAL ROSE
1. Select the note icon (folded rectangle) from the tool palette.
2. Click on the diagram to draw the note.
3. Select the attachment icon (dashed line) from the tool palette.
4. Click on the note and drag the attachment line to the appropriate element.

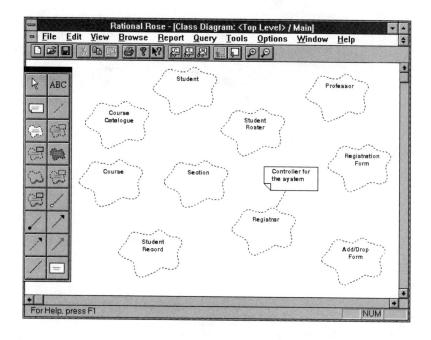

THE MODEL DICTIONARY

EVERY MODELING ELEMENT (class, attribute, operation, relationship) in Rational Rose contains a specification. The model dictionary is the sum of all the specifications for each modeling element in the system. As soon as a class is created, its definition (textual description of purpose and responsibilities) should be added to the class specification. Additional information about the class is entered into the specification as analysis proceeds.

ADDING THE DEFINITION TO THE
CLASS SPECIFICATION IN RATIONAL ROSE

1. Double-click to make the Class Specification window visible.
2. Click inside the documentation field and type the definition of the class.
3. Click the OK button to close the Class Specification window.

The Class Specification for the Student class is shown below.

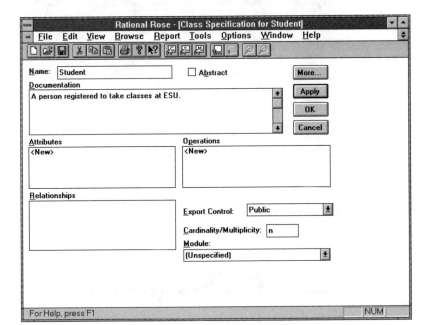

UPDATED CONTEXT DIAGRAM

ADDITIONAL SYSTEM INPUTS and outputs may be identified by looking at the use cases and scenarios for the major actors that interact with the system under development. The initial context diagram should be updated to reflect any additional information. The updated context diagram for the course registration problem follows on page 41.

SUMMARY

USE CASES AND scenarios are a powerful way to begin the analysis phase of system and software development. The external actors are explored to discover their primary uses of the system. Each use of the system is expanded to form a web of scenarios—the primary scenario and the representative exceptions to that case. Each noun in the scenario is examined, and candidate classes are defined. The candi-

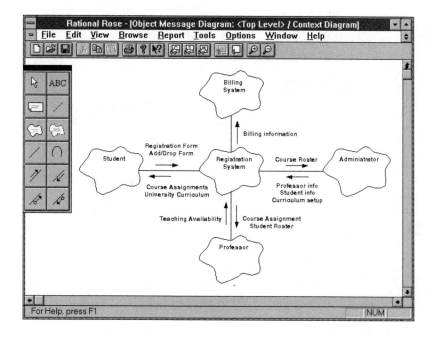

date classes along with their definitions are entered into a Rational
Rose class diagram.

GLOSSARY

CLASS

A collection of objects with the same structure and behavior.

CLASS DIAGRAM

A diagram used to show the existence of classes and their
relationships in the logical design of a system.

SCENARIO

An outline of events that elicits some system behavior.

SPECIFICATION

Additional nongraphical information for each element (class, relationship, etc.) in a class and scenario diagram.

USE CASE

A scenario that begins with some user of the system initiating some transaction or sequence of interrelated events (as defined by Ivar Jacobson).

Chapter 5

Analysis: Attributes and Operations

BEHAVIOR AND STRUCTURE

THE BEHAVIOR OF an object is described by the operations of its class. All instances of a class have access to the operations of that class. The structure of an object is described by the attributes of the class—each attribute is a property or characteristic of the class. Each instance of a class has a value for every attribute defined for the class. The attributes and operations defined for a class are domain-specific; that is, they have meaning and utility within the application that is being developed.

As with classes, style guides should be created and followed for defining attributes and operations. In this case study, attributes and operations start with a lowercase letter and underscores are not used. Names composed of multiple words are closed up (no space within them), and the first letter of each additional word is capitalized (e.g., numberStudents). Care should be taken to ensure that appropriate style guides are followed for all defined attributes and operations. This provides consistency across the classes, which leads to more maintainable models and code.

DIAGRAMMING SCENARIOS AND DESCRIBING OBJECT BEHAVIOR

AT THIS POINT, it is useful to have a picture showing the object interactions described in the scenarios for the system. There are two ways to diagram scenarios: object message diagrams and message trace diagrams (either one may be used). Each diagram shows the object involved in the scenario and the messages sent between the objects. The objects may be external to the system (actors interacting with the system) or internal to the system. The messages are typically behavior or operations of the receiving class.

A message trace diagram is a tabular way to show a scenario. Each object that participates in the scenario is drawn as a vertical line, and the messages between the objects are shown as horizontal lines from sender to receiver.

CREATING MESSAGE TRACE

DIAGRAMS IN RATIONAL ROSE

1. Choose Scenario Diagram from the Browse menu option.
2. Double-click on < New > to display the New Scenario window.
3. Type the name of the scenario in the Name field of the New Scenario window.
4. Confirm that Message Trace is the selected option.
5. Click the OK button.

The New Scenario window is shown below.

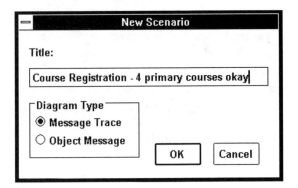

CREATING OBJECTS AND MESSAGES IN

MESSAGE TRACE DIAGRAMS IN RATIONAL ROSE

1. Click to select the object icon (solid cloud) from the tool palette.
2. Click on the diagram window.
3. Type the name of the object in the cloud.
4. Double-click on the object to make the Object Specification window visible.
5. Attach the object to a class by selecting the class name from the Class: pulldown menu.
6. Repeat the above steps for each object in the scenario.

7. Click to select the message icon (arrow) from the tool palette.
8. Move the mouse pointer to the line for the sending object, click, and drag the line to the receiving object.
9. To create the message and make the message an operation of the receiving class, click the right mouse button on the receiving class.
10. Select either an existing operation or select a new operation.
11. If a new operation is selected, type the name of the operation in the Name field of the Operation Specification.
12. To make the newly created operation visible, click the right mouse button, and select the operation from the list of operations.

The message trace diagram for the scenario of registering for a course when the four primary choices are valid is shown below.

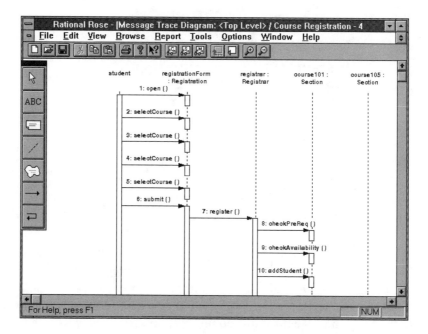

An optional script that explains the scenario in words may be added to a message trace diagram to provide additional documentation for the scenario diagram. A script may be written in free-form text, structured text, or the chosen implementation language.

CREATING SCRIPTS IN RATIONAL ROSE
1. Select the text icon (ABC) from the tool palette.
2. Click on the diagram and type the text for the script.
3. Resize the text if necessary.
4. Click on the text, depress the shift key, and click on the message for the script.
5. Choose the Attach Script menu option from the Edit menu.

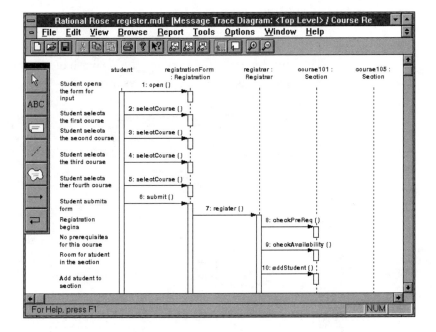

An object message diagram is an alternate way to show a scenario. Each participating object is represented as a solid cloud. A link, which indicates a communication path, is a solid line between objects. Messages are shown attached to the object links. Object message diagrams do not contain scripts, however; therefore any script added to a message trace diagram will not appear in a corresponding object message diagram.

CREATING OBJECT MESSAGE DIAGRAMS FROM
MESSAGE TRACE DIAGRAMS IN RATIONAL ROSE

1. Choose the Scenario Diagrams option from the Browse menu.
2. Open the message trace diagram by selecting the diagram from the list of scenario diagrams and clicking the OK button.
3. Choose the Create Object Diagram option from the Browse menu or press the F5 key.

The object message diagram follows.

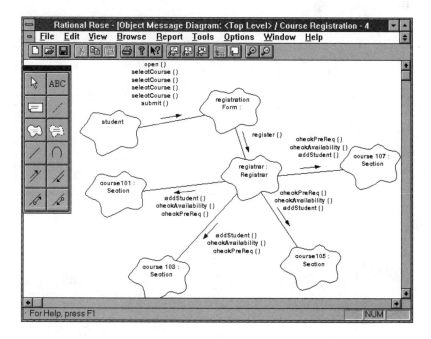

Object message diagrams can also be created from scratch. A message trace diagram can then be created from the object message diagram by selecting the Create Message Trace Diagram option from the Browse menu or pressing the F5 key.

CREATING OBJECT MESSAGE
DIAGRAMS IN RATIONAL ROSE

1. Choose Scenario Diagram from the Browse menu.
2. Double-click on < New > to display the New Scenario window.
3. Select the Object Message Diagram Type radio button.
4. Type the name of the scenario in the Title field of the New Scenario window.
5. Click the OK button.

The New Scenario window for an Object Message Diagram follows.

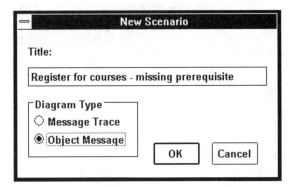

CREATING OBJECTS AND MESSAGES IN OBJECT
MESSAGE DIAGRAMS IN RATIONAL ROSE

1. Click to select the object icon (solid cloud) from the tool palette.
2. Click on the diagram window to draw the object.
3. Type the name of the object inside the cloud.
4. Double-click on the object to display the Object Specification window.
5. Attach the object to a class by selecting the class name from the Class: pulldown menu.
6. Repeat the above steps for each object in the scenario.

7. To add a link for the message, select the link icon from the tool palette (solid line), click on the object sending the message, and drag the link to the receiving object.
8. To add the message arrow to the link, select the icon (arrow) from the tool palette and click on the link.
9. To create the message and make it an operation of the receiving class, click the right mouse button on the message arrow.
10. Select either an existing operation or a new operation.
11. If a new operation is selected, type the name of the operation in the Name field of the Operation Specification.
12. To make the newly created operation visible, click the right mouse button and select the operation from the list of operations.

The object message diagram follows.

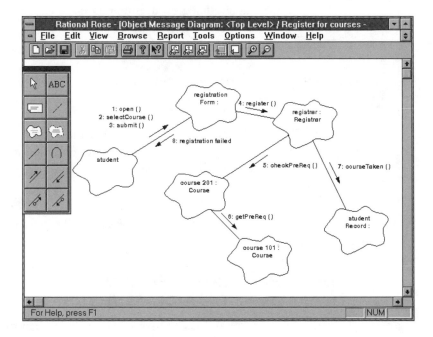

SPECIFYING ATTRIBUTES FOR CLASSES

MANY OF THE attributes of a class appear in the problem statement. They may also be discovered when supplying the definition of a class. Knowledge of the domain can reveal additional attributes of the class. As attributes are created, their definitions should be captured. Other information, such as the data type, is specified during design.

We can define the following attributes for the registration problem:

> Student—name, address, phoneNumber, studentID number, major, year
> Course—title, description, section, startTime, endTime, daysOffered, location
> Professor—name, employeeID number, department, phoneNumber
> RegistrationForm—date, semester
> Add/dropForm—date, semester, signature
> CourseCatalog—semester, dateIssued
> StudentRecord—dateLastUpdated

CREATING ATTRIBUTES IN RATIONAL ROSE
1. Display the Class Specification window by double-clicking on the class.
2. Double-click on < New > in the Attributes field.
3. Type the attribute name and its documentation in the Class Attribute specification window.

The name attribute for the Student class follows on page 53.

SHOWING ATTRIBUTES AND OPERATIONS ON A CLASS DIAGRAM

AS ANALYSIS PROGRESSES, it may become helpful to be able to view certain attributes and operations directly on a diagram. This is especially useful for customer reviews.

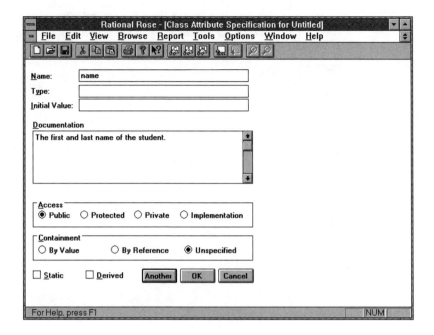

 SHOWING ATTRIBUTES IN RATIONAL ROSE

1. Position the mouse pointer near the class and click the right mouse button.
2. Select the Edit Compartment option.
3. Select the attributes to be shown on the class diagram and click the > > button to move the selected items to the Show Items field.
4. Click the OK button.

The following diagram shows the attributes and operations for the RegistrationForm class.

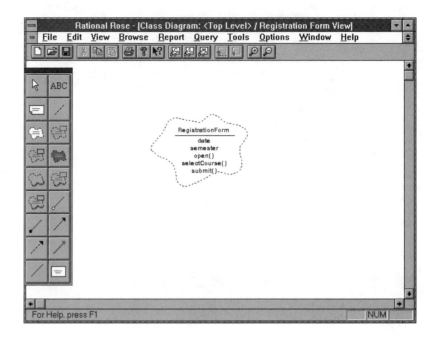

SUMMARY

THE BEHAVIOR OF an object is described by the operations of the class. All instances of the class have access to the operations of the class. Behavior is discovered by the messages between objects defined in the scenarios for a project. An attribute is a property or characteristic of a class. Each instance of a class has a value for every attribute defined for the class. Many attributes are found in the problem statement. They may also be determined when supplying the definition of a class. Domain knowledge also adds to the definition of attributes for classes.

GLOSSARY

ATTRIBUTE

> A property or characteristic of a class.

MESSAGE TRACE DIAGRAM

> A graphical depiction of a scenario. It is a tabular diagram that shows objects on vertical lines and the messages between the objects on horizontal lines.

OBJECT MESSAGE DIAGRAM

> A graphical depiction of a scenario. Objects are shown as solid clouds, and messages are shown attached to links between the objects participating in the scenario.

OPERATION

> Work that one object performs upon another, or itself, in order to elicit a reaction; the behavior of the class.

Chapter 6

Analysis: Defining Relationships

OBJECT INTERACTION

ALL SYSTEMS ARE made up of many classes and objects. System behavior is the result of the collaboration of the objects in the system. Their collaboration is often referred to as one object "sending a message" to another object. Relationships provide the conduits for object interaction. Two main types of relationships are discovered and defined during analysis: associations and aggregations.

DEFINING ASSOCIATIONS

AN ASSOCIATION IS a bidirectional semantic connection between two classes. Data may flow in either direction. An association is represented as a line drawn between the associated classes.

CREATING ASSOCIATIONS IN RATIONAL ROSE
1. Select the association icon (straight line) from the tool palette.
2. Click on one of the associated classes.
3. Drag the association line to the other associated class.

An association may be named, and its name is usually an active verb or verb phrase that communicates the meaning of the relationship. It is important to note that the name of the association is optional; we use them if they are needed to add clarity to the model.

NAMING ASSOCIATIONS IN RATIONAL ROSE
1. Double-click on the association line to bring up the Association Specification window.
2. Enter the name of the association in the Name field of the Association Specification.
3. Click the OK button.

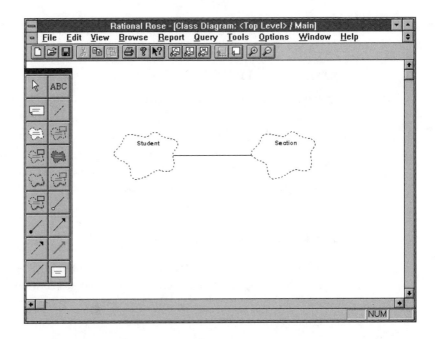

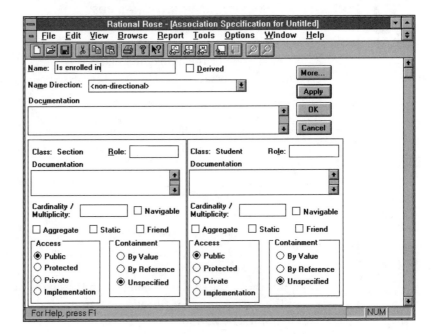

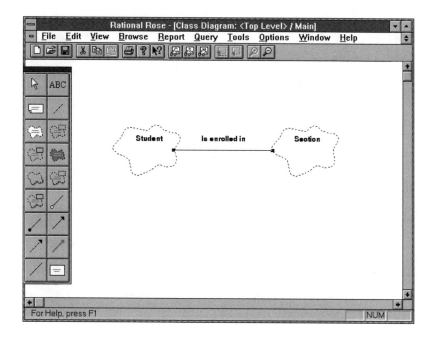

DEFINING ROLE NAMES

ROLES CAN BE used instead of association names. A role name is a
noun or adjective that denotes the role an object plays in an association, and it is placed on the association line near the class that
it modifies. A role name may be placed on one or both ends of an
association line. It is not necessary to have both a role name and
an association name.

CREATING ROLES IN RATIONAL ROSE

1. Double-click on the association line to bring up the
   Association Specification window.
2. Enter the name of the role in the Role field of the
   Association Specification.
3. Click the OK button.

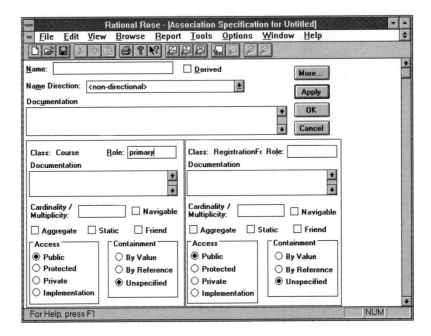

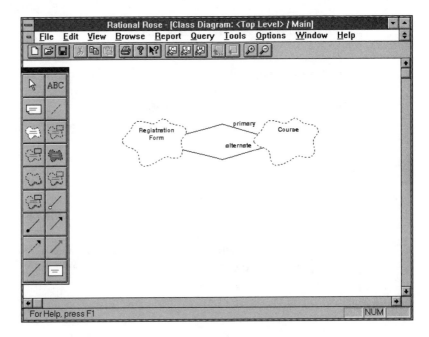

DEFINING AGGREGATIONS

AN AGGREGATION IS a stronger form of association that shows the relationship between a whole and its parts, known as a "has a" or containment relationship. Aggregations typically have dependent life cycles. An aggregation is drawn as a line with a filled-in ball at the "whole" part of the relationship. Aggregations are not usually named; they are read using the words "has" or "contains."

CREATING AGGREGATIONS IN RATIONAL ROSE

1. Select the aggregation icon (line with a filled-in circle at one end) from the tool palette.
2. Click on the class playing the role of the "whole" and drag the aggregation line to the class playing the role of the "part."

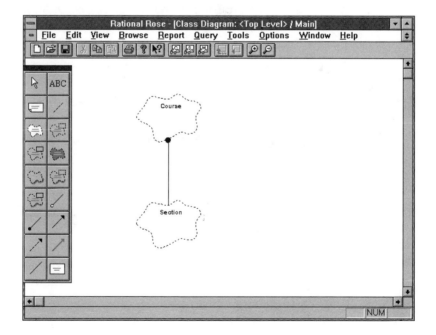

MULTIPLICITY FOR ASSOCIATIONS AND AGGREGATIONS

MULTIPLICITY REFERS TO the number of instances that participate in a relationship. There are two multiplicity indicators for each association or aggregation—one at either end of the relationship. The multiplicity is shown on the class diagram for each association and aggregation. Some common multiplicity indicators follow:

1	Exactly one	n	Zero or more
0..n	Zero or more	1..n	One or more
0..1	Zero or one	5..8	Specific range (5, 6, 7, or 8)
4..7,9	Combination (4, 5, 6, 7, or 9)		

SHOWING MULTIPLICITY IN RATIONAL ROSE

1. Double-click on the association or aggregation link.
2. Enter the multiplicity in the Cardinality/Multiplicity field of the Association specification.
3. Click on the OK button.

Multiplicity is shown in the following diagram.

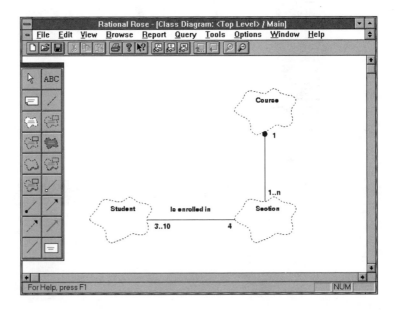

ATTRIBUTED ASSOCIATIONS

A MANY-TO-MANY relationship may have structure and behavior that belongs to the relationship itself. This information is captured in an attributed association, which is a class attached to the relationship by a dashed line.

CREATING ATTRIBUTED
ASSOCIATIONS IN RATIONAL ROSE

1. Select the class icon (dashed cloud) from the tool palette.
2. Click on the diagram to draw the class.
3. Enter the attributes and operations for the attributed class.
4. Select the attachment icon (dashed line) from the tool palette.
5. Click on the attributed class and drag the attachment line to the relationship.

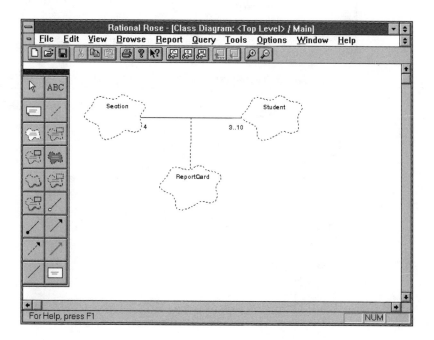

REFLEXIVE ASSOCIATIONS AND AGGREGATIONS

MULTIPLE OBJECTS BELONGING to the same class may have to communicate with one another. This is shown on the class diagram as a reflexive association or aggregation.

CREATING REFLEXIVE RELATIONSHIPS IN RATIONAL ROSE

1. Select the association (or aggregation) icon from the tool palette.
2. Click on the class and drag the association (or aggregation) line to a place on the class diagram.
3. Click on the diagram to begin to form the association.
4. Click on the class to complete the association.
5. Double-click on the relationship to bring up the Association Specification.
6. Enter the role names and multiplicity for each end of the reflexive association (or aggregation).

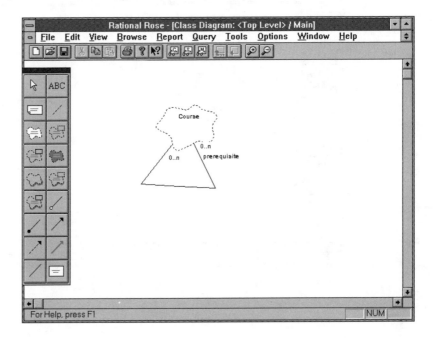

RELATIONSHIPS IN THE ESU COURSE REGISTRATION PROBLEM

RELATIONSHIPS AMONG CLASSES are determined by examining the problem statement and by looking at interactions contained in the identified scenarios. A message can be sent from one object to another only if their respective classes are connected by an association or aggregation. If a class is important to the system only because it is "part of" or "contained in" another class, then we should model the relationship as an aggregation. Otherwise, a simple association is all that we need at this time. Be especially careful to look for reflexive relationships. The next step is to add multiplicity to each relationship in the initial model of the system. Each association and aggregation must be examined to determine how many instances are involved in the relationship. Conversations with customers and domain experts along with examination of the identified scenarios provide good inputs for this process.

Examining the "Course Registration—4 Courses Okay" scenario reveals the following relationships:

> RegistrationForm and Registrar
> Registrar and Course
> Registrar and StudentRecord
> Registrar and StudentRoster
> Course and Course (reflexive)
> Course and Section

Each relationship is modeled as an association at this time, although they may mature into "has" relationships as the analysis and design progresses. The class diagram follows at the top of page 68.

Each scenario should be examined to add additional relationships to the diagram. If association names are needed to communicate the meaning of the relationships, they are added to the diagram. Finally, multiplicity indicators are also added. The initial class diagram is updated to reflect the added relationships and multiplicity indicators. The updated class diagram follows at the bottom of page 68.

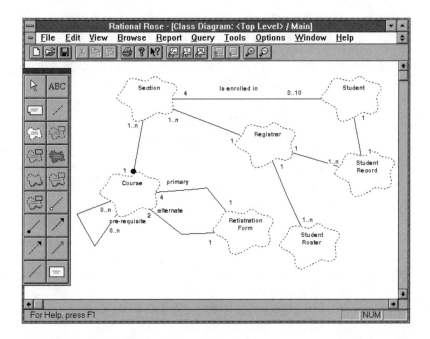

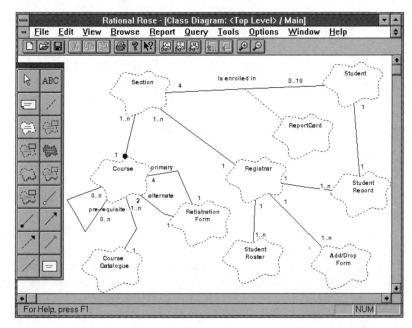

SUMMARY

RELATIONSHIPS PROVIDE THE mechanism for object interaction. There are two main types of relationships discovered during analysis: associations and aggregations. An association is a bidirectional connection between two classes. Messages and data may flow in either direction. An association is drawn as a line between the associated classes. An aggregation is a stronger form of association that shows the relationship between a whole and its parts. It is known as a "has a" or containment relationship. Multiplicity is the number of instances that participate in a relationship. There are two multiplicity indicators for each association or aggregation—one at either end of the relationship.

GLOSSARY

AGGREGATION
> A stronger form of association that shows the relationship between a whole and its parts.

ASSOCIATION
> A bidirectional semantic connection between two classes.

MULTIPLICITY
> The number of instances that participate in a relationship. Multiplicity indicators are shown at each end of a relationship line.

ROLE
> A description of how an object participates in a relationship.

Chapter 7

Analysis: Inheritance

■

Using Generalization and Specialization to Find
Superclasses and Subclasses

■

Inheritance in the ESU Course Registration Problem

■

Summary

■

Glossary

USING GENERALIZATION AND SPECIALIZATION TO FIND SUPERCLASSES AND SUBCLASSES

INHERITANCE DEFINES A relationship among classes where one class shares the structure and/or behavior of one or more classes. A hierarchy of abstractions is created in which a subclass inherits from one or more superclasses. With single inheritance, only one superclass exists, while multiple inheritance allows more than one superclass. Inheritance is also called an "is-a" or "kind-of" hierarchy. Attributes and operations are defined at the highest level in the hierarchy at which they are applicable, which allows all lower classes in the hierarchy to inherit them. There are two ways to find inheritance in any system: generalization and specialization.

Generalization provides the ability to create superclasses that encapsulate structure and behavior common to several classes. This is very common in domain analysis endeavors, because the classes that currently exist are those that model the real world. Classes are examined for commonality of structure (attributes) and behavior (operations). You should be on the lookout for synonyms, since attribute and operation names are expressed in natural language and the commonality might be hidden. Additionally, examine behavior which at first glance may seem specific but in reality may be generalized. For example, in one use case, the student "selects" a course from the course catalogue, and in another use case the student "picks" a course from the course catalogue. If behavior is extracted from each use case, then the course catalogue would have two operations; select and pick. Because the behavior is the same, however, only one operation is needed.

Specialization provides the ability to create subclasses that represent refinements in which structure and behavior may be added or modified. This method of finding inheritance comes into play if a class library already exists, which may be either an internal library or a purchased library. Subclasses are added to specialize the behavior of an existing class.

There is no limit to the number of classes allowed in an inheritance hierarchy. However, practical experience has shown that typical C++ class hierarchies contain between three and five layers, while Smalltalk applications may be a bit deeper.

Inheritance is shown by an arrow that points from the subclass to the superclass.

CREATING INHERITANCE IN RATIONAL ROSE

1. Select the inheritance icon (solid arrow) from the tool palette.
2. Click on the subclass.
3. Drag the inheritance arrow from the subclass to the superclass.

An inheritance relationship is shown in the following figure.

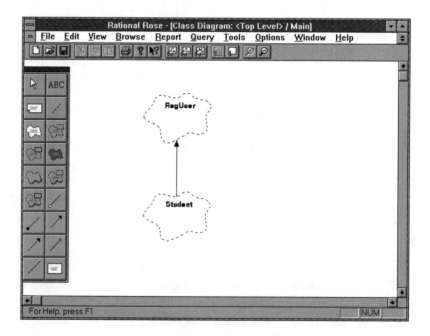

INHERITANCE IN THE ESU COURSE REGISTRATION PROBLEM

AT THIS TIME only generalization is used to find inheritance, since there are no preexisting classes for our problem. Specialization may come into play at a later date. By examining the classes, you can see that there is commonality between the Student class and the Professor class. Both classes are abstractions of real people and contain the following attributes in common: name, address, and phoneNumber. The Student class contains a studentID, and the Professor class contains an employeeID. These attributes can be generalized and renamed IDNumber. A RegUser superclass is created to hold the common structure, while the unique features remain in the Student and Professor classes. The Student and Professor classes are added as subclasses to the RegUser hierarchy. It is important to note that although there is a real-life Registrar, the class in the system does not contain any attributes or operations in common with the Student or Professor; therefore, the Registrar class is not a subclass of RegUser. The RegUser hierarchy is shown in the figure below.

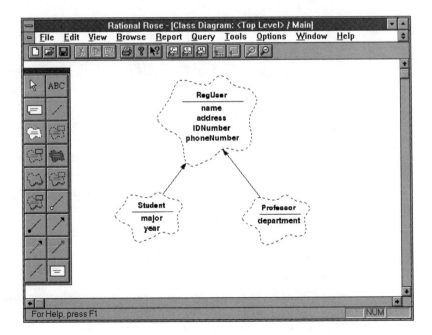

Using the same strategy of examining existing classes, a Form hierarchy may also be created. Here the RegistrationForm and the Add/DropForm both contain the student name, date, and semester and the operations open, close, and submit. The Form hierarchy is shown in the following figure.

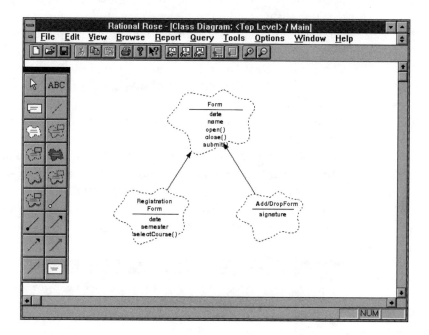

SUMMARY

INHERITANCE PROVIDES THE ability to create a hierarchy of classes that share common structure and behavior. The term *superclass* is used for the class holding the common information. The descendants are called *subclasses*. There are two ways to find inheritance in any system: generalization and specialization.

Generalization provides the ability to create superclasses to encapsulate structure and behavior that is common to several classes. Specialization provides the ability to create subclasses that represent refinements in which structure and behavior from the superclass are added or refined. Inheritance is shown by an arrow that points from the subclass to the superclass.

GLOSSARY

CLASS LIBRARY
>A library consisting of classes that may be used by other developers.

GENERALIZATION
>Process used to create superclasses that encapsulate structure and behavior common to several classes.

INHERITANCE
>A relationship among classes, where one class shares the structure and/or behavior defined in one or more other classes.

SPECIALIZATION
>Process used to create subclasses that represent refinements in which structure and/or behavior are added or modified.

SUBCLASS
>A class that inherits from one or more classes.

SUPERCLASS
>The class from which another class inherits.

Chapter 8

Analysis: Object Behavior

MODELING OBJECT BEHAVIOR USING STATE TRANSITION DIAGRAMS

USE CASES AND scenarios provide a way to describe system behavior, that is, the interaction between objects in the system. Objects with significant dynamic behavior require further analysis of their behavior. A state transition diagram shows the states of a single object, the events or messages that cause a transition from one state to another, and the actions that result from a state change. Each object has a limited number of states, and the object can be in only one state at a given time.

A transition represents a change from an originating state to a successor state (which may be the same as the originating state). An action can accompany a transition.

There are two kinds of transitions: automatic and nonautomatic. An automatic transition occurs when the activity of the originating state completes—there is no event associated with the transition. A nonautomatic transition is caused by an event (originating either from another object or from outside the system). Either type of transition may also contain a guard condition that allows the transition to occur only if the condition evaluates to true. Both types of transitions are considered to take zero time and cannot be interrupted.

Behavior that occurs inside a state is called an *activity*. An activity starts when the state is entered and either completes or is interrupted by an outgoing transition.

State transition diagrams are not created for every class in the system; they are only created for classes with significant dynamic behavior. Interaction diagrams can be studied to determine the dynamic objects in the system—ones that receive and send many messages. State transition diagrams are also useful to investigate the behavior of an aggregate "whole" class.

Developers must be careful to stay in an analysis frame of mind, concentrating on the *what* of the problem and not the *how* of the problem.

CREATING STATE TRANSITION
DIAGRAMS IN RATIONAL ROSE

1. Click to select the class that needs a state transition diagram.
2. Select State Diagram from the Browse menu.
3. The State Diagram window is opened.
4. Select the state icon (rounded rectangle) from the tool palette.
5. Click on the state transition diagram to draw the state.
6. Repeat steps 4 and 5 to draw a second state.
7. Select the transition icon (arrow) from the tool palette.
8. Click on the state and drag the arrow to the next state.

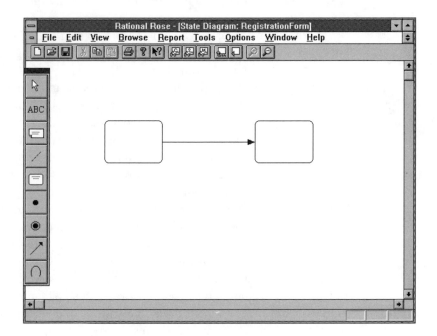

START AND STOP STATES

TWO SPECIAL KINDS of states are added to the state transition diagram. The first is a start state. Each diagram must have one and only one start state, since the object must be in a consistent state when it is created. A start state is shown in the following diagram.

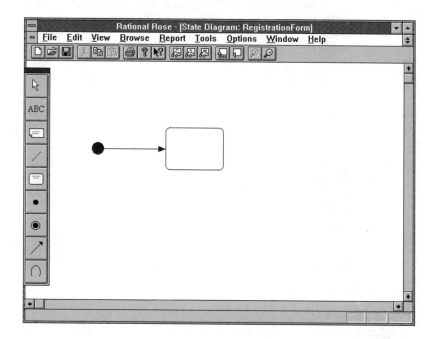

CREATING START STATES IN RATIONAL ROSE

1. Select the state icon (rounded rectangle) from the tool palette.
2. Click on the state transition diagram to draw the state.
3. Select the start icon (filled-in circle) from the tool palette.
4. Click on the state transition diagram to draw the start icon.
5. Select the transition arrow (arrow) from the tool palette.
6. Click on the start icon and drag the arrow to the state.

The second special state is a stop state. An object can have multiple stop states. A stop state is shown in the following diagram.

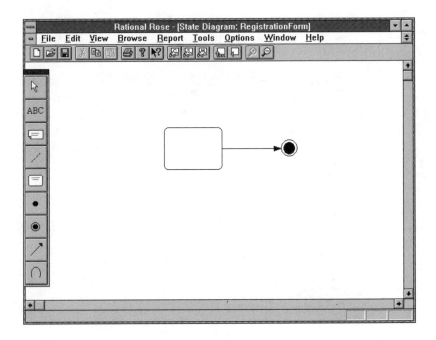

 CREATING STOP STATES IN RATIONAL ROSE

1. Select the state icon (rounded rectangle) from the tool palette.
2. Click on the state transition diagram to draw the state.
3. Select the stop icon (bull's eye) from the tool palette.
4. Click on the state transition diagram to draw the stop icon.
5. Select the transition arrow (arrow) from the tool palette.
6. Click on the state and drag the arrow to the stop icon.

 **CREATING ENTRY ACTIONS, EXIT ACTIONS,
AND ACTIVITIES IN RATIONAL ROSE**

1. Double-click on the state to make the State Specification window visible.
2. Double-click on < New > to make the State Action window visible.

3. Select the appropriate radio buttons for Type and When:
   Action and On Entry to create an entry action;
   Action and On Exit to create an exit action;
   Action and Entry until Exit to create an activity.
4. Enter the name of the action in the Action field.
5. Click the OK button.

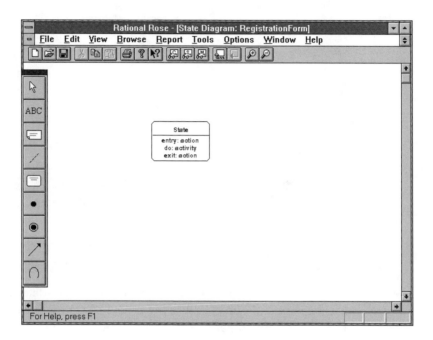

 **NAMING TRANSITIONS, CREATING GUARD CONDITIONS,
AND CREATING ACTIONS IN RATIONAL ROSE**
1. Double-click on the transition to make the State Transition Specification window visible.
2. Enter the name of the transition event in the Event field.
3. Enter the name of the condition in the Condition field.
4. Enter the name of the action in the Action field.
5. Click the OK button.

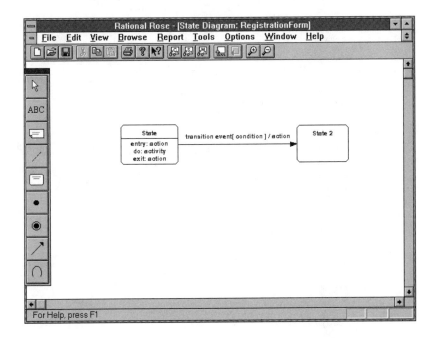

STATE TRANSITION DIAGRAMS FOR THE ESU COURSE REGISTRATION PROBLEM

BY EXAMINING THE message trace diagrams, we can determine that the RegistrationForm class has the following states: creating the form, accepting primary courses, accepting alternate courses, saving the form, and submitting the form. The state transition diagram is shown in the following figure on page 87.

SUMMARY

CLASSES THAT EXHIBIT significant dynamic behavior are analyzed in depth by creating state transition diagrams, which show all the states of an object, the events that the object receives, and the resulting actions that are taken. Transition events along with their accompanying actions are considered to take zero time and cannot be interrupted. States, along with their accompanying activities, can be interrupted.

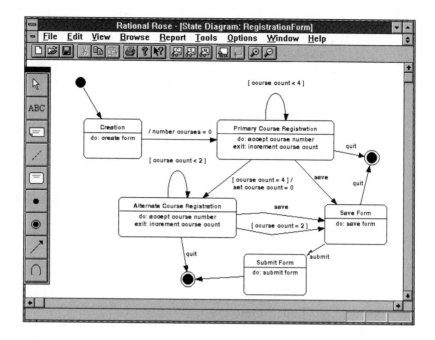

GLOSSARY

ACTION

> Behavior that accompanies a transition event. An action is considered to take zero time and cannot be interrupted.

ACTIVITY

> Behavior that occurs while in a state. An activity can be interrupted by a transition event.

AUTOMATIC TRANSITION

> Transition that occurs automatically after the activity within the originating state is completed.

GUARD

> A condition that must evaluate as true if a specified transition is to occur.

STATE

> The cumulative results of the behavior of an object; one of the possible conditions in which an object may exist.

STATE TRANSITION DIAGRAM

> Diagram used to show the state space of a given class, the events that cause a transition from one state to another, and the actions that result from a state change.

TRANSITION

> The passing of an object from one state to another state.

Chapter 9

Analysis: Consistency Checking and Model Validation

THE NEED FOR CONSISTENCY
CHECKING AND MODEL VALIDATION

CONSISTENCY CHECKING IS needed because several views of the system are under development in parallel. In this book, the static view (class diagram) and the dynamic view (object message diagrams and message trace diagrams) have been discussed individually. In developing a real system, however, both views are under development concurrently and must be cross-checked to ensure that different assumptions or decisions are not being made in different views.

Model validation is needed to check that the class structure under development will be sufficient to implement a system meeting the needs of the customer. In other words, model validation verifies that all requirements have been captured and represented correctly.

Checking and validation do not occur during a separate phase or a single step of the analysis process. They are integrated throughout the analysis phase and continue throughout the life cycle of the system under development. They are best accomplished by a small team (5–6 people at most) comprised of analysts, customers or customer representatives, and test personnel.

SCENARIO WALKTHROUGH

A PRIMARY METHOD of consistency checking is to walk through each high-risk scenario as represented by an object message or message trace diagram. In the course registration problem, the scenarios that deal with database interaction should be checked. Since each message represents behavior of the receiving class, verify that each message is captured as an operation on the class diagram. Verify that two interacting ojects have a pathway for communication via either an association or an aggregation. Be especially careful to check for reflexive relationships that may need to be created. These relationships are easy to miss during analysis. Reflexive relationships are needed when multiple objects of the same class interact during a scenario.

Make sure that each class represented on the class diagram participates in at least one scenario. For each operation listed for a class, verify that either the operation is used in at least one scenario or it is needed for completeness. Finally, make sure that each object included in the dynamic model belongs to a class on the class diagram, unless it represents an external entity.

EVENT TRACING

FOR EVERY MESSAGE shown in object message diagrams and message trace diagrams, verify that an operation on the sending class is responsible for sending the event and that an operation on the receiving class expects the event and handles it. Verify that there is an association or aggregation on the class diagram between the sending and receiving classes, and add the relationship to the class diagram if it is missing. Finally, if a state transition diagram for the class exists, verify that the event is represented on the diagram for the receiving class, since this diagram must show all the events that a class may receive.

REVIEW OF THE MODEL DICTIONARY

EACH CLASS SHOULD be defined in the model dictionary. Check for uniqueness of class names, and review all class definitions for completeness. Make sure that all attributes and operations also have complete definitions. Finally, check that all standards, format specifications, and content rules established for the project have been followed. Since the model dictionary is one of the primary inputs to design, it should be made consistent before work on the problem progresses.

REQUIREMENTS TRACEABILITY

MODEL VALIDATION INCLUDES tracing each requirement to the class(es) and operation(s) that satisfy it. Requirements are generally traced to classes and scenarios. For small or informal projects, the requirements may be added to the model dictionary entry for each class. For larger or more formal projects, a commercial requirements tool or database management system may be used.

SUMMARY

CONSISTENCY CHECKING AND model validation must be performed throughout the life cycle of any project. Consistency checking is needed because several views of the system are under development in parallel, and care must be taken to ensure that the models correspond. There are three ways to perform consistency checking; scenario walkthroughs, event tracing, and review of the model dictionary.

Model validation is needed to verify that the class structure under development will be sufficient to implement a system that meets the needs of the customer. The main way to validate the set of models is to trace the system requirements. Most requirements are traced only to the class level and not to individual operations.

GLOSSARY

CONSISTENCY CHECKING

> The process of ensuring that information in both the static view of the system (class diagram) and the dynamic view of the system (object diagram and/or message trace diagram) are telling the same story.

MODEL VALIDATION

> The process of ensuring that all requirements have been captured in the set of models for the system under development.

Chapter 10

Design: Defining an Architecture

THE NEED FOR ARCHITECTURE

REGARDING THE NEED for architectural development, Grady Booch writes, "Every project requires this phase. Establishing a sound architectural foundation is absolutely essential to the success of an object-oriented project. Some teams try to ignore this phase, either because they are in such a rush to get a product out quickly they feel they don't have time to architect, or because they don't believe that architecting provides them any real value. Either way, the resulting head-long rush to code is always disastrous: fail to carry out this step properly, and your project will likely experience software meltdown."[1]

The architecture of an object-oriented system is organized in terms of distinct layers and partitions. A layer denotes classes at the same level of abstraction; it is a horizontal slice. A partition denotes a vertical slice. Each layer represents a coherent abstraction and contains a well-defined and controlled interface. Additionally, each layer of the system is built upon well-defined and controlled facilities at lower levels of abstraction.

The architecture establishes the basic structure of the system. Executable prototypes of the architecture are built to verify that the design decisions made are correct. "Building something executable is absolutely essential, because it forces the development team to validate their design assumptions in the harsh light of reality."[2]

THE "4 + 1" VIEW OF ARCHITECTURE

SOFTWARE ARCHITECTURE IS not a one-dimensional thing—it is made up of concurrent multiple views. The diagram on page 98 shows the five views of software architecture.[3]

---

[1] Booch, Grady. *Object Solutions.* Redwood City, Calif.: Addison-Wesley, 1995.

[2] Ibid.

[3] Kruchten, Philippe. *Software Architecture and Iterative Process.* Santa Clara, Calif.: Rational Software Corporation, 1994.

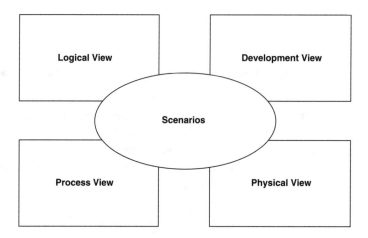

The logical view addresses the functional requirements of the system—what the system should provide in terms of services to its users. The logical architecture is captured in class diagrams that contain the classes and relationships that represent the key abstractions of the system.

The process view focuses on process decomposition. The system is decomposed into a set of independent tasks that are grouped into processes. A task is an independent thread of control that may be individually scheduled on a process node. Additionally, tasks can be explicitly addressed by other tasks. The process architecture also takes into account some nonfunctional requirements, such as performance, reliability, scalability, integrity, system management, and synchronization. Module diagrams are created to show the different modules that make up the process architecture of the system.

The development view of the architecture concerns itself with the actual software module organization within the development environment. The software is packaged into subsystems that are organized in a hierarchy of layers, and each layer has a well-defined interface. The development architecture takes into account mostly derived requirements related to ease of development, software management, reuse, and constraints imposed by the toolset or the programming language. Subsystems are added to the module diagrams created for the process view of the architecture.

The physical view of the architecture involves mapping software to processing nodes. The physical architecture takes into account requirements such as system availability, reliability, performance, and scalability. Process diagrams are created to show the different processors and devices in the system.

Scenarios are the glue that holds the views together—they demonstrate and validate the logical, process, development, and physical views. A scenario is an operational behavior characterized by externally visible stimulus and response of the final system. Scenarios are decomposed across the various objects (classes), processes, layers, subsystems, and modules to show how those various design elements interact to produce the desired behavior. Scenarios are represented by either message trace diagrams or object message diagrams.

Each view should be independent, so that changes in one view do not affect another view. Such independence allows parallel development to occur. The following figure shows the relationship between the different views of the system.

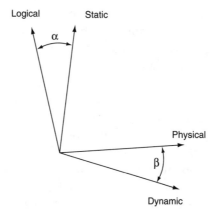

For a small project, the logical and development views can be completely identical; that is, one class corresponds to one module, and one class category to one library. Similarly, the process and physical views may be identical for smaller systems, consisting of a simple mapping such as one process per processor. A greater separation between the views becomes apparent in larger, more complex systems.

THE ARCHITECTURE TEAM

EACH PROJECT SHOULD have a chief architect who may be assisted by a small team. "The main activities of the architect include the definition of the architecture of the software, the maintenance of the architectural integrity of the software, the assessment of the technical risks of the project, the definition of the order and content of the successive iterations along with the planning of each iteration, providing consulting to various design, implementation, integration, and quality assurance teams and assisting in providing future market directions."[4]

CLASS CATEGORIES

A CLASS CATEGORY is a logical collection of classes that are themselves highly cohesive, but are loosely coupled to other classes. Class categories may be used to represent the major architectural pieces of a system. In Booch notation, a class category is represented by a rectangle, and each one must have a unique name.

A "uses" relationship between categories is drawn to show communication between the categories. There should be low coupling between the categories of any system. If every category uses every other category, then the logical architecture probably needs improvement. Certain categories, however, such as foundation classes (sets, lists, etc.) are used by every category in the system. A category that is used by all or most of the categories is considered to be a *global* category.

A top-level class diagram may be constructed that contains only class categories. Such a class diagram reveals the logical architecture of the system, that is, the layers and partitions that compose it.

THE CATEGORIES IN THE ESU COURSE REGISTRATION PROBLEM

BY EXAMINING THE classes and scenarios developed during analysis, we can create the following categories to represent the logical archi-

---

[4] Kruchten, Philippe. *Software Architecture and Iterative Development.* Santa Clara, Calif.: Rational Software Corporation, 1994, p. 53.

tecture of the course registration system; Database (handle persistent objects in the system), Registration User Interface, and the Registration System. Other categories will be added to the system as the design progresses.

CREATING CLASS CATEGORIES IN RATIONAL ROSE
1. Select the category icon (rectangle) from the tool palette.
2. Click on the class diagram.
3. Type the name of the category inside the category rectangle.

The top-level class diagram is shown in the following figure.

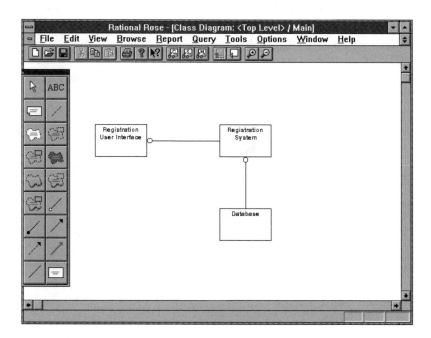

TACTICAL DESIGN DECISIONS

TACTICAL DESIGN FOCUSES on decisions regarding common standards, polices, and practices. "Poor tactical design can ruin even the most profound architecture, and so the team must mitigate this risk by explicitly identifying the project's key policies."[5] Some common policies involve the selection of an implementation language, persistent data storage, the look and feel of the user interface, error handling, and communication mechanisms. Classes and categories are added to the system to implement and enforce the decisions made.

TACTICAL DESIGN DECISIONS IN THE COURSE REGISTRATION PROBLEM

SINCE MOST OF the development team had prior experience with the C++ language and because this system will eventually be expanded to include other university functions, C++ was the language chosen by the architecture team. The architecture team also decided that a particular set of graphical user interface (GUI) widgets should be used to control the look and feel of the user interface; therefore, they added a category called GUI Widgets to the model. The database persistence strategy chosen by the architecture team is to use a corresponding database class (shadow class) for each persistent class in the system. Although other strategies that mainly involve the use of inheritance could have been chosen, the team chose this strategy because expertise in implementing this method of persistence already existed and the team felt that it involved the least amount of risk. The shadow classes are added to the Database category. Additionally, it was decided to make use of the C++ features of catch and throw for exceptions. Rather than making each class be responsible for knowing how to catch and throw exceptions, however, the team added a category called Error Handling to the model. Finally, the foundation classes chosen for this system are the Booch Components. Since the Error Handling category and the Booch Components category are used by every other category in the system, they are global categories.

---

[5] Booch, Grady. *Object Solutions.* Redwood City, Calif.: Addison-Wesley, 1995.

MAKING A CATEGORY GLOBAL IN RATIONAL ROSE
1. Click on the category in the class diagram.
2. Choose Specification from the Browse menu to open the Category Specification window.
3. Check the global box.
4. Click the OK button.

The updated top-level class diagram follows.

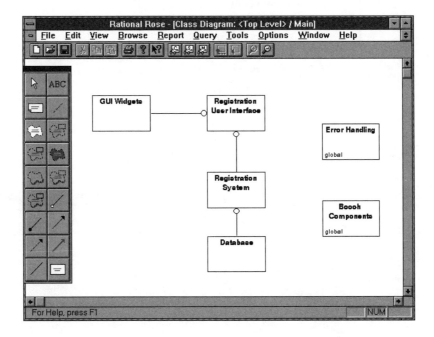

MOVING CLASSES TO CATEGORIES

ONCE THE CATEGORIES have been created, the original classes in the class diagram must be moved to the appropriate categories. Most of the classes discovered during analysis will belong to the application category (in this case the Registration System). Other classes are added to represent the architectural and tactical design decisions made during this phase of development.

In the course registration problem, the Form hierarchy belongs to the Registration Interface category, and all the other classes belong to the Registration System category. Additionally, the interface classes that show the communication between the categories are added to the category class diagram.

MOVING CLASSES TO A CATEGORY IN RATIONAL ROSE

1. Select the classes and relationships to be moved from the class diagram.
2. Choose Cut from the Edit menu.
3. Double-click on the category to open it.
4. Choose Paste from the Edit menu.
5. With the classes still selected, choose Relocate from the Edit menu. (All other diagrams are updated to show that the moved entities now "belong to" the target category).

The class diagram for the Registration Interface category follows.

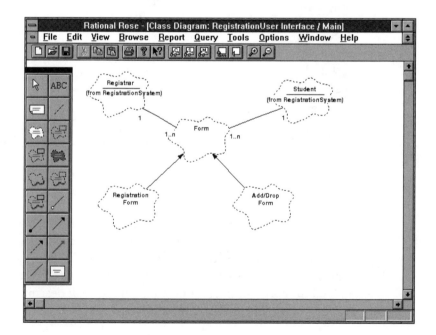

SUBSYSTEMS

CLASS CATEGORIES REPRESENT the logical partitioning of the system—the software components that comprise the solution. Subsystems represent the physical partitioning of the system—the physical arrangement of the software components. In general, a class category corresponds directly to a subsystem. Sometimes a one-to-one mapping is not possible. For example, categories may be merged to keep closely communicating objects together, or subsystems may be added to implement low-level functionality not represented during analysis (i.e., communication for distributed systems).

SUBSYSTEMS IN THE COURSE REGISTRATION PROBLEM

THERE IS A one-to-one mapping for most of the categories in the course registration problem. The only subsystem that contains two categories is the GUI subsystem. The GUI Widgets category and the Registration User Interface categories have been combined because the classes in these two categories are tightly coupled.

DRAWING SUBSYSTEMS IN RATIONAL ROSE
1. Choose Module Diagram from the Browse menu.
2. Select the subsystem icon (ellipse) from the tool palette.
3. Click on the module diagram.
4. Type the name of the subsystem inside the subsystem icon.

The top-level subsystem diagram follows on page 106.

THE PROCESS DIAGRAM

DURING DESIGN, THE last diagram to be started is the process diagram. This diagram shows the physical processors in the system,

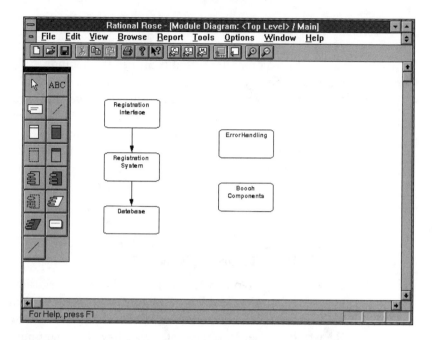

their devices, and the connections between processors. A processor
is a piece of hardware capable of executing programs, and a device
is a piece of hardware that cannot execute a program. A connection
indicates a communication link, usually by means of direct hardware coupling. The process diagram allows the architecture team to
understand the system topology and aids in mapping subsystems
to executable processes. Issues such as processor architecture, speed,
and capacity along with interprocess communication bandwidth/
capacity, physical location of the hardware, and distributed processing techniques all come into play.

THE PROCESS DIAGRAM FOR THE
COURSE REGISTRATION PROBLEM

AFTER STUDYING THE subsystems defined for the course registration
problem, examining existing hardware, and estimating the load on
the system during the course registration period, the architecture
team decided that they would need two processors for the system:
one to handle the registration system and its user interface and the

other to handle the database. The registration system processor will be connected to three devices: one in the main building, one in the dorm, and one in the library.

CREATING THE PROCESS DIAGRAM IN RATIONAL ROSE
1. Choose Process Diagram from the Browse menu.
2. Select the processor icon (shaded rectangle) from the tool palette.
3. Click on the process diagram.
4. Type the name of the processor inside the processor icon.
5. Select the device icon (unshaded rectangle) from the tool palette.
6. Click on the process diagram.
7. Type the name of the device inside the device icon.
8. To connect each processor to its device(s), select the connection icon (line) from the tool palette, click on the processor icon in the diagram, and drag the connection to the appropriate device.

The initial process diagram follows on page 108.

SUMMARY

THE PURPOSE OF the design phase is to create an architecture for the implementation and to establish the common tactical policies to be used throughout the system. Software architecture is not one-dimensional; it is made up of concurrent multiple views: logical, development, process, and physical. Scenarios are the glue that hold the four views together. Good architectures are constructed in well-defined layers of abstraction, so that there is a clear separation between the interface and implementation of each layer. Tactical design focuses on decisions regarding common standards, policies, and practices. Class categories are created to show the architectural layout of the system and the results of the tactical decisions made. Finally, it is during this phase that the team begins to move from the logical models to physical models. Module diagrams are created to show sub-

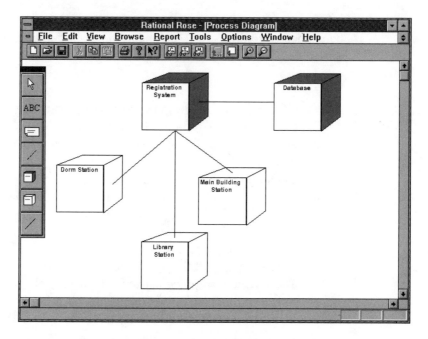

systems that are the physical implementations of the categories. Process diagrams are created to show the hardware configuration to be used for the system under development.

GLOSSARY

ARCHITECTURE

The logical and physical structure of a system, forged by all the strategic and tactical design decisions made during development.

CLASS CATEGORY

A logical collection of classes; some of these are visible to other class categories, and others are hidden. The classes in a class category collaborate to provide a set of services.

LAYER
> The collection of class categories or subsystems at the same level of abstraction.

PROCESS DIAGRAM
> A diagram used to show the allocation of processes to processors in the physical design of a system.

SUBSYSTEM
> The physical implementation of a category.

TACTICAL DESIGN DECISION
> A design decision that has architectural implications.

TOP-LEVEL CLASS DIAGRAM
> A class diagram that shows the major categories of a system.

Chapter 11

Design: Iteration Planning

■

Planning Iterations Using Use Cases

■

Iteration Planning for the Course Registration Problem

■

Summary

■

Glossary

PLANNING ITERATIONS USING USE CASES

PLANNING ITERATIONS IS typically the last step of the design phase. During this step, the iterations to be developed during the evolution phase are documented using a project planning tool. The output of this phase is a release plan that prescribes schedules for all the increments of the system. "Such a plan must identify a controlled series of architectural releases, each growing in its functionality and ultimately encompassing the requirements of the complete production system."[1] In addition to the release plan, a testing and integration strategy is developed. "For most projects, plan on about five (plus or minus two) intermediate releases during evolution."[2]

The scenarios developed during analysis are the main input to this phase of design. The scenarios are examined and prioritized according to risk, importance to the customer, and the need to develop certain basic scenarios early. This task is best accomplished with a team made up of a domain expert, analysts, the architect, and testing personnel. "Scenarios should be grouped so that for each release, they collectively provide a meaningful chunk of the system's behavior and additionally require the development team to attack the project's next highest risks."[3]

ITERATION PLANNING FOR THE COURSE REGISTRATION PROBLEM

THE FOLLOWING SCENARIOS were identified during the analysis of course registration at ESU.

Student: Request curriculum list
                  Register for courses

---

[1] Booch, Grady. *Object Solutions*. Redwood City, Calif.: Addison-Wesley, 1995.

[2] Ibid.

[3] Ibid.

	Drop a course
	Add a course
Administrator:	Set up curriculum
	Add another section to a course
	Cancel a course
Professor:	Indicate courses to be taught
	Request student list
	Add a course
	Drop a course

The biggest risk identified for the course registration problem is the use of a relational database to store the curriculum for a given semester. Prototypes done during analysis and design showed that information stored in a relational database could be retrieved in a timely manner, so that performance requirements could be satisfied. These prototypes began to mitigate the identified risk. The first release of the system (which continues to mitigate the database risk) should implement the "Set up Curriculum" use case (Administrator), and the "Indicate Courses to Be Taught" use case (Professor).

The team decided that the other releases would be as follows:

Release 2

Request Curriculum List
Register For Courses (Student)

Release 3

Add Another Section To A Course (Administrator)
Cancel A Course (Administrator)

Release 4

Drop A Course For A Student
Add A Course For A Student

Release 5

Request Student List
Drop A Course For A Professor
Add A Course For A Professor

SUMMARY

RELEASE PLANNING IS the last step in the design phase of the macro process. The output of this phase is a schedule of the architectural releases to be developed during the evolution phase of development. Scenarios developed during analysis are the primary input to the release-planning activity. The scenarios are examined and prioritized according to risk, importance to the customer, and the need to develop certain basic scenarios early. The planning activity is generally performed by a small team made up of domain experts, analysts, the system architect, and testing personnel.

GLOSSARY

ARCHITECTURAL RELEASE

An iteration to be developed during the evolution phase that encompasses the behavior of several scenarios.

Chapter 12

Design: Use of Commercial Class Libraries

PICKING A COMMERCIAL CLASS LIBRARY

THE FASTEST WAY to obtain reuse in any project is to buy reusable classes. There are many commercial libraries on the market today for everything from GUI widgets to communication mechanisms to libraries geared toward certain vertical markets. Care must be taken when selecting the class libraries to be used in the project. Libraries should be evaluated using, at a minimum, the following criteria:

- Completeness: The library must provide a complete family of classes that provide all the capability the library claims to have.

- Adaptability: All platform-specific aspects must be clearly identified and isolated.

- Efficiency: Components must be easily assembled, must impose minimal run-time and memory overhead, and must be more reliable than hand-built mechanisms.

- Simplicity: The library must use a clear and consistent organization that makes it easy to identify and select appropriate classes.

- Documentation: Each class must be fully documented— developers will build their own class rather than reuse one that is hard to understand.

ADDING THE COMMERCIAL CLASSES TO THE MODEL

COMMERCIAL CLASS LIBRARIES can be reverse-engineered using the Rational Rose Analyzer. This tool reads C++ code and generates a .mdl file for Rational Rose. In the course registration problem, the Booch Components library was chosen as the foundation class library. Now is the time to incorporate the library into the registration model. By incorporating the library into the model under development, the designer can graphically show how the classes identified during analysis interact with the commercial classes.

SETTING UP A PROJECT IN THE
RATIONAL ROSE/C++ ANALYZER

1. Start the Rose/C++ Analyzer by double-clicking on the program icon.
2. Choose the New option from the File menu.
3. Click the Caption button, type the name in the Caption window, and click the OK button.
4. Click the Directories button to display the Project Directory List window.
5. Select the desired directory and click the appropriate button: Add Current, Add Subdirs or Add Hierarchy. Repeat this process until all directories have been added.
6. Click the OK button.
7. Click the Extensions button to display the Project File Extensions window.
8. Select the appropriate extensions and click the OK button.
9. Click the Files button to bring up the Project Files window.
10. To analyze all the files in the directory, click the Add All Files button.
11. To analyze only selected files, select the file and click the Add Files button.
12. Click the OK button.
13. The project is now set up. Choose the Save or the Save As option from the File menu to save the project.

The following figure on page 121 shows the Analyzer window.

ANALYZING FILES WITH THE
RATIONAL ROSE/C++ ANALYZER

1. Click on the files to be analyzed.
2. Choose the Code Cycle option from the Actions menu. When the program asks if the files can be updated, click the

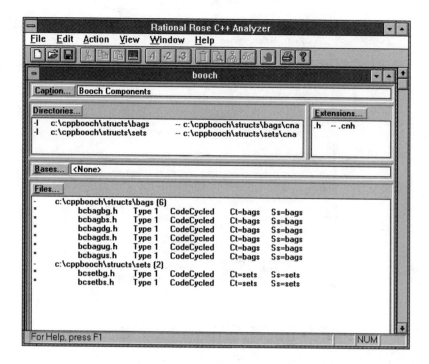

Yes button. This inserts the markers that are needed by the code-generation capabilities of Rose.

3. When the Analyzer is finished, the window is updated to show that the files have been code cycled as shown on page 121.

EXPORTING FILES FROM THE ROSE/C++ ANALYZER

1. Choose the Export Options option from the Edit menu.
2. Select the needed options.
3. Click the OK button.
4. Select the classes to be exported.
5. Choose the Export to Rose option from the Actions menu.
6. Click the OK button (or the Overwrite button if the model already exists).

Now that a model has been created by the Analyzer, you can view it by loading the .mdl file into Rose.

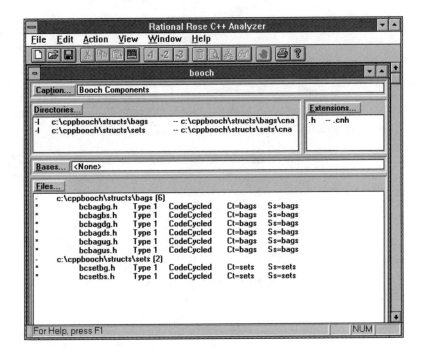

 VIEWING THE REVERSE-ENGINEERED
MODEL IN RATIONAL ROSE

1. In Rose, choose Open from the File menu.
2. Select the .mdl file generated by the Analyzer and click the OK button. The model contains categories for each directory. These categories should be recategorized as subcategories of the Booch Components category.
3. Select all the categories and choose the Cut option from the Edit menu to remove them from the diagram.
4. Create a new category called Booch Components.
5. Double-click on the Booch Components category to open it.
6. Choose the Paste option from the Edit menu to paste the previously cut categories.
7. With the categories still selected, choose the Relocate option from the Edit menu.

The diagrams follow.

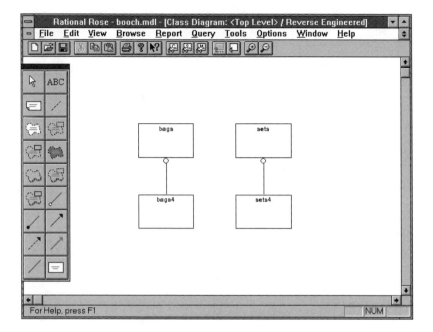

The next step involves making the Booch Components category a controlled unit. A .cat file will be created, which can be loaded into other models.

MAKING CONTROLLED UNITS IN RATIONAL ROSE
1.   Click on the category to be controlled to select it.
2.   Choose the Units/Control option from the File menu.
3.   Type the name of the .cat file in the File Name For Unit window
4.   Click the OK button. The unit is created and marked with a U in an octagon.
5.   The control unit adornment can be turned off by choosing the Display command from the Options menu.

The top-level class diagram follows.

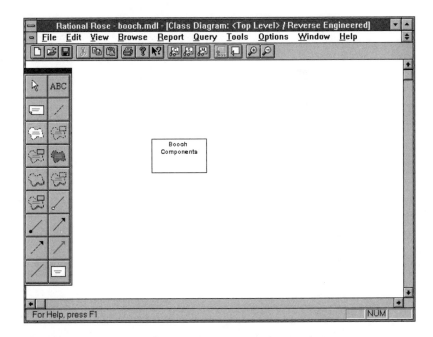

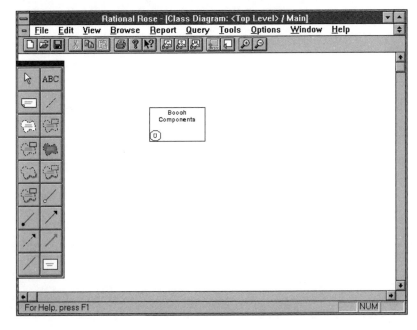

The preceding process only has to be done once. The resulting
.cat file is saved and can be loaded into any model.

LOADING CONTROL UNITS IN RATIONAL ROSE
1. Choose the Open option from the File menu.
2. Select the name of a .mdl file and click the OK button.
3. Select the Units/Load option from the File menu.
4. Select the .cat file to load.
5. Click the OK button.
    NOTE: If you have a place-holder category for the class
    library, Rose will ask if you want to overwrite the category.
    Click the Yes button to replace the category.

The top-level diagram for the course registration problem
follows.

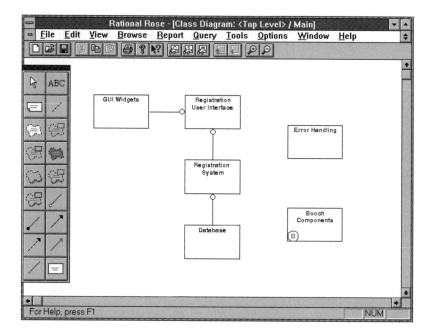

SUMMARY

THE FASTEST WAY to obtain reuse in any project is to buy reusable classes. There are many commercial libraries on the market today for everything from GUI widgets to communication mechanisms to libraries geared toward certain vertical markets. Commercial class libraries can be reverse-engineered using the Rational Rose Analyzer. This tool reads C++ code and generates a .mdl file for Rational Rose. A category for the class library can be created, made into a controlled unit, and imported into the model for the current project. This provides the ability to graphically show how the classes identified during analysis interact with the commercial classes.

GLOSSARY

CLASS LIBRARY
    A collection of classes purchased from a vendor.

REVERSE-ENGINEER
    The ability to create a class diagram starting with existing code.

Chapter 13

Evolution: Building an Architectural Release

APPLICATION OF THE MICRO PROCESS

THE ARCHITECTURAL RELEASES defined during the design phase are developed during the micro process. It is important to note that the code developed during this phase is production-quality code (fully implemented, tested, and documented). Each architectural release incrementally adds functionality to the system under development. The development of the releases is managed by the application of the micro process, which represents the daily activities of the individual developer or a small team of developers.

IDENTIFYING CLASSES AND OBJECTS

AT THIS STAGE, the developer is focusing on the slice of the system being built to support the current architectural release. The first architectural release to be built implements the Set Up Curriculum use case. The scenario for this use case follows:

Administrator creates a course.
Administrator sets the course name, time, section, and location.
Administrator saves the course.
Administrator adds the course to the course catalogue.

The classes identified from these scenarios during analysis are Course and CourseCatalogue. The class diagram follows on page 130.

IDENTIFYING CLASS AND OBJECT SEMANTICS

THE MESSAGE TRACE diagrams created during analysis are the primary input to this phase of evolution. Additional scenarios—especially secondary scenarios (What if...?)—are also considered.

The development team for the course registration problem has determined that a window must exist to allow the administrator to set up the curriculum. They have adopted a model-view-controller style of architecture, and this information is added to the message

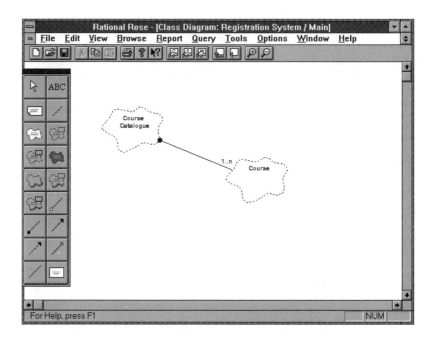

trace diagrams. The updated message trace diagram for the Set Up Curriculum use case follows at the top of page 131.

This scenario leads to the discovery of two additional classes: CurriculumWindow and CurriculumController. They are implementation classes; that is, their creation is based on the design of the system. The diagram is examined to discover additional behavior and relationships for the classes involved in the scenario. The class diagram is updated to show the results. The figure shown at the bottom of page 131 shows the updated class diagram.

Secondary scenarios for the Set Up Curriculum use case would also be considered—"not enough information supplied by the administrator" and "course created but not added to the catalogue" are two of the secondary scenarios that may be considered.

The micro process continues until the team experiences the law of diminishing returns—no new classes found, no new behavior discovered, and the set of implementation classes seems to be complete.

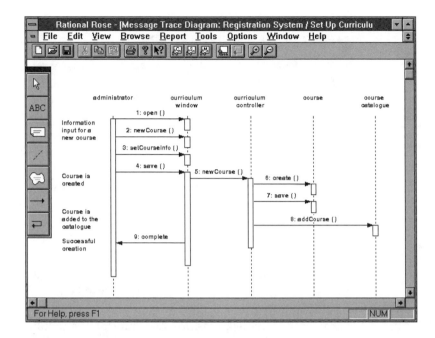

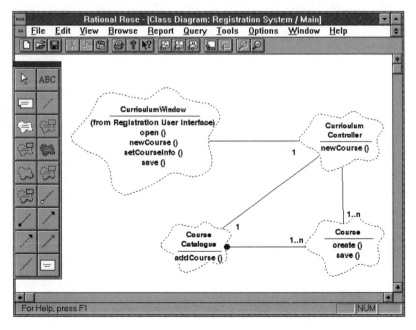

IDENTIFYING CLASS AND OBJECT RELATIONSHIPS

ASSOCIATIONS ARE AN analysis concept that shows a relationship between two classes. They cannot be implemented. During design and evolution, each association is matured into either a has or a uses relationship.

A "has" relationship is also referred to as a containment relationship— it implies that the containing class has intrinsic knowledge of the contained class. During this phase of the micro process, each "has" relationship is further refined to either containment by value or containment by reference. Containment by value implies dependent lifetimes, while containment by reference does not mandate dependent lifetimes. The other type of relationship is a "uses" relationship. In a "uses" relationship, the using class does not have intrinsic knowledge of the location of the used class—it must be told where the object is located. Typically, the used object is passed as a parameter to one of the methods of the using class. Examination of message trace diagrams provides information that helps the designer determine the best design for the relationships in the system.

The implementation of multiplicity for relationships is also decided during this phase. A multiplicity of 1 is usually an embedded object (containment by value), or a reference or pointer (containment by reference). Multiplicity of more than 1 is typically implemented using a container class (e.g., a set or a list). Again, the list may be an embedded object (containment by value) or a pointer to the container (containment by reference).

Continuing with the Set Up Curriculum use case, we see a relationship between the curriculum window and the controller. Another team has developed the CurriculumWindow class and the SAVE button on the window sends the newCourse message to the controller. Due to the design and the GUI Widgets chosen to implement the window, this relationship is a "uses" relationship (the actual design and implementation of the Window class is beyond the scope of this text). The controller sends the courseComplete message back to the Window, but this has been implemented as the return from the newCourse message. Therefore, this relationship is unidirectional (from the CurriculumWindow to the Curriculum-Controller). The class diagram is updated to show this information.

CHANGING RELATIONSHIPS IN RATIONAL ROSE
1. Select the relationship line.
2. Choose the Change Into option from the Edit menu.
3. Select the new relationship type.

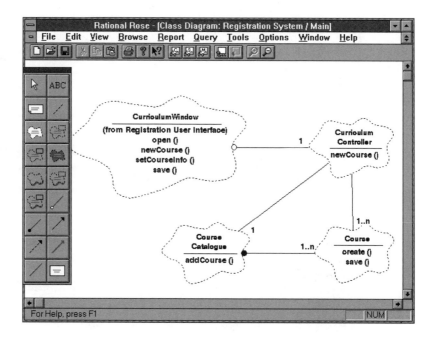

There is a one-to-many relationship between the CourseCatalogue class and the Course class. Again, this relationship is unidirectional (from the catalogue to the course). A single linked list will be used to implement the "many" part of this relationship. This single list is owned by the catalogue and is implemented as a "has-by-value" relationship. In the Booch Components foundation library, this class is an instantiation of the template class BC_TSingleList template class. The actual relationship must be moved from the

Course class to the instantiated list class, and the multiplicity
changes to 1 (the CourseCatalogue contains exactly one CourseList).

CREATING PARAMETERIZED CLASS
INSTANTIATIONS IN RATIONAL ROSE

1. Select the instantiated parameterized class icon (class with
   a solid rectangle in the upper left corner) from the tool
   palette.
2. Click on the class diagram window.
3. Type the name of the class in the instantiated class icon.
4. Select the instantiation relationship (dotted arrow) from the
   tool palette.
5. Drag the instantiation arrow from the instantiated class to
   the parameterized class.

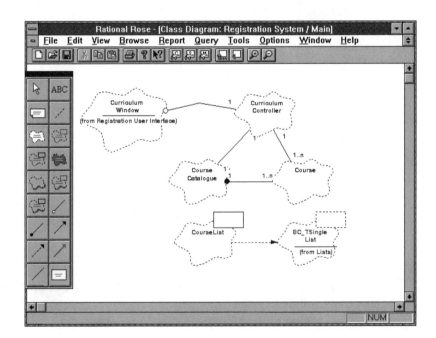

MOVING RELATIONSHIPS IN RATIONAL ROSE
1. Select the relationship line.
2. Point to the end of the relationship to be moved and drag the relationship to the new class.

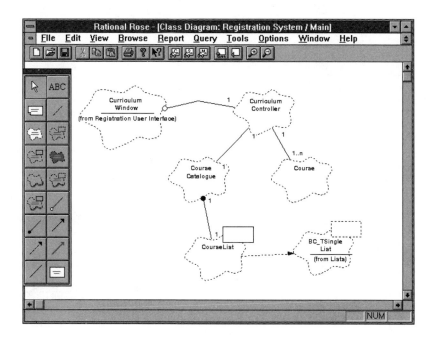

CREATING "HAS-BY-VALUE"
RELATIONSHIPS IN RATIONAL ROSE
1. Select the desired has relationship line.
2. Double-click on the relationship line to display the Relationship Specification window.
3. Select the Containment By Value radio button.
4. Click the OK button.

The modified class diagram follows.

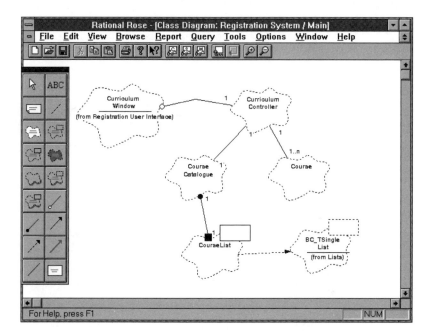

The CurriculumController needs to send the addCourse message to the CourseCatalogue. Because the controller has knowledge of the catalogue object, the relationship is a "has" relationship. Both the controller object and the catalogue object exist independently, so the relationship is a "has-by-reference" relationship. This is shown in the following class diagram shown on page 137.

The next relationship to tackle is the association between the controller and the course classes. In order to determine how to design and implement this relationship, the designer must decide which class creates the Course object. The controller could create the object and send it to the catalogue. This design would create a "has-by-value" relationship between the controller and the course and a "uses" relationship between the catalogue and the course. Another solution is to have the catalogue create the object and send it back to the controller (so that the controller can tell the object to save itself). Here, there is a "has" relationship between the catalogue and the course and a "uses" relationship between the controller and the course.

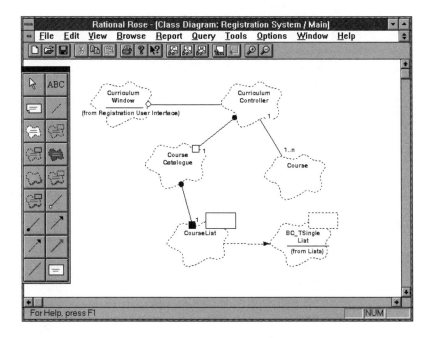

Which way is correct? They both are. Which way is better? It depends. By looking at more scenarios, and figuring out how persistence will be implemented, the designer will determine which design is best. To continue this discussion is beyond the scope of this book, but the bottom line is that the model is updated during this phase of evolution to reflect the design of the system. For the purpose of this book, the first solution has been chosen, and the updated model is shown in the following figure on page 138.

SPECIFYING CLASS AND OBJECT IMPLEMENTATIONS

THE NEXT PHASE of the evolution process is to specify class and object implementations: attribute data types, method function prototypes, adding additional methods to the class (i.e., constructors, destructors, helping methods), and method algorithms. The documentation supplied at analysis should also be reviewed and updated if necessary.

Our discussion concentrates on the Course class. The documentation supplied during analysis for this class does not need any addi-

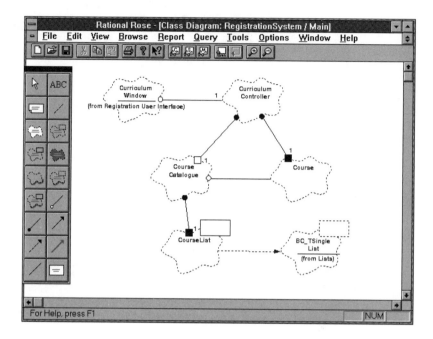

tional information. The following attributes have been defined: description, daysOffered, startTime, endTime, location, section, and title. A data type must be supplied for each attribute, and this is accomplished via the Attribute Specification window. The attributes are either character strings or amounts of time. The Booch Components library contains a string template class and a time class. A CharacterString class can be instantiated from the BC_TString class and used as the implementation type for any attribute that is a character string. The class BC_CTime can be used for any attribute dealing with time.

The attribute specification for the description attribute is shown in the following figure on page 139.

Method function prototypes must also be updated for each method in each class in the model. The new information generally emerges as the designer examines message trace diagrams and object message diagrams and designs the relationships among the classes.

The Course class has the following methods defined: addStudent, courseAvailable, create, and save. The courseAvailable method

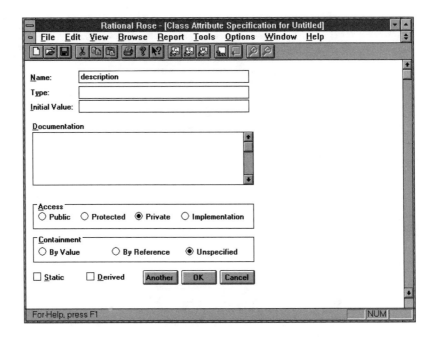

does not have any parameters, but it does return a Boolean value. The parameters and return type are added to the operation specification, which is shown in the following figure on page 140.

The final step is to add the methods that every good C++ class needs—for example, constructors, destructors, and copy constructors. These methods can be added by hand, but this requires a lot of typing. The ability to add such methods to a class is provided as a feature of the Rose code generator to make this task easier.

CODE GENERATION

RATIONAL ROSE HAS a very powerful C++ code-generation capability. Options for the code generator are set using the Properties/Edit Properties option from the Tools menu. There are properties associated with the model, the class, "has" relationships, attributes, and operations. The properties applying to the model as a whole involve file names, default container names, and the placement of the generated code. Class properties involve the generation of constructors,

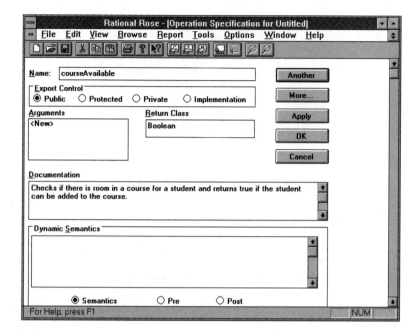

destructors, copy constructors, equality operators, and get/set methods. The property set for "has" relationships deals with the construction of get/set methods, the visibility of the methods, and the
container class to be used. Operation properties deal with the operation kind (common, virtual, abstract, static, or friend) and allow the
operation to be made constant.

These property sets may be edited, and new sets may be created
to specify the C++ features needed for the project. Two files are
generated for each class: a header (.h) file and a specification (.cpp)
file.

GENERATING CODE IN RATIONAL ROSE
1. Click on a class or category.
2. Edit the property sets or create new property sets if
    necessary by clicking on the appropriate element
    (class, relationship, or operation) and choosing the
    Properties/Edit Properties option from the Tools menu.

3. Choose the Generate C++ Code option from the Tools
    menu; code is generated, and all messages are written to
    the log.

The code generated for the Course class (using the default property sets) is shown in Appendix C.

The final step of the process is to add the method code to the
preserved regions in the .cpp file and test the classes. Each class
should be tested by itself (Does it do what it is supposed to do?) and
as a class participating in a scenario (Are all collaborations correct?).

DOCUMENTATION FOR THE RELEASE

DECISIONS MADE REGARDING the design of the release are captured
in the model and in the specifications for each modeling element. A
written narrative that explains the key scenarios and the class diagram is also helpful. It is especially useful to developers if the system
must be modified.

SUMMARY

DURING THIS PHASE of development the system is evolved as a series
of architectural releases. The code generated is of production quality
(fully implemented, tested, and documented). Each release incrementally adds functionality to the system under development. This
phase is managed by following the steps in the micro process:

- Identify classes and objects—identify the classes to be
  implemented for the current architectural release

- Identify class and object semantics—look at additional
  scenarios to find implementation classes

- Identify class and object relationships—look at the
  additional scenarios to verify relationships found
  during analysis and add new relationships for the
  implementation classes

■ Identify class and object implementations—refine associations into "has" or "uses" relationships, specify attribute data types and method function prototypes, add manager (constructor, destructor, etc.) and helping methods, specify method algorithms, and generate the code for the release.

Documentation for the release is contained in the model, the element specifications, and optionally in a larger design document that includes a narrative format.

GLOSSARY

"HAS-BY-REFERENCE" RELATIONSHIP
A containment relationship where the containing class and the contained class exist independently.

"HAS-BY-VALUE" RELATIONSHIP
A containment relationship where the containing class and the contained class have dependent lifetimes.

IMPLEMENTATION CLASS
Class added to the system during the design and evolution phases of development. These classes are usually not part of the domain but are necessary to implement software capabilities (e.g., a linked list class).

MODEL-VIEW-CONTROLLER ARCHITECTURE
A popular architecture for application software containing model classes (typically classes discovered during analysis), view classes (classes responsible for screen presentation), and controller classes (classes that control the interface between the model and view classes).

PARAMETERIZED CLASS
A class that serves as a template or blueprint for other classes.

"USES" RELATIONSHIP
> A relationship where the using class does not have any intrinsic knowledge of the used class—the using class is told the location of the used class.

Chapter 14

Evolution: Building the Next Release

■

Using Reverse-Engineering to Set the Stage
for the Next Architectural Release

■

Summary

■

Glossary

USING REVERSE-ENGINEERING TO SET THE STAGE FOR THE NEXT ARCHITECTURAL RELEASE

THE MODEL MUST be updated to reflect any design-level changes made to the code (e.g., helping methods added, new classes added) while implementing the current release. Rather than updating the model by hand, we can use the reverse-engineering capability of Rose to generate a model based on the current implementation, and then incorporate this information into the design model.

REVERSE-ENGINEERING USING THE ROSE/C++ ANALYZER

1. Set up a Rose/C++ project; remember to include all directories referenced by your code.
2. Tip: Set up a base project for the C++ libraries and any class library used.
3. Select the files to be analyzed.
4. Choose the Code Cycle option from the Actions menu.
5. Export the code to Rose, making sure you export to a new model name. *Do not overwrite* your design model.

The course registration problem uses the Booch Components class library. The project booch.pjt was created to reverse-engineer this library, and it can be used as a base project here.

The Analyzer window is shown in the figure at the top of page 148.

Once the files are analyzed, the information is exported to Rose. The model created by the program is course.mdl.

This information must now be imported into the original design model for the course registration system.

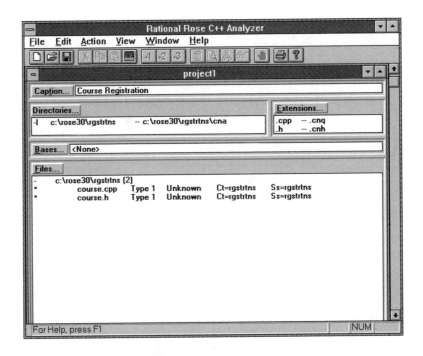

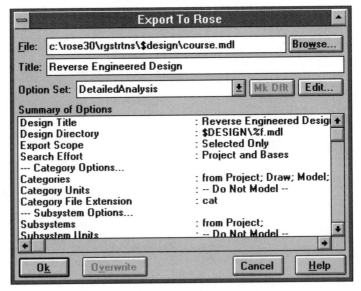

UPDATING MODELS IN RATIONAL ROSE

1. Choose the Open option from the File menu.
2. Choose the original design model and click the OK button.
3. Choose the Update option from the File menu.
4. Enter the name of the reverse-engineered model just created by the analyzer in the File Name field on the Update Model From window.

The following figures show the original and updated class diagrams.

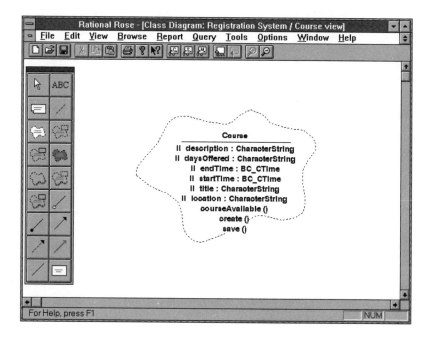

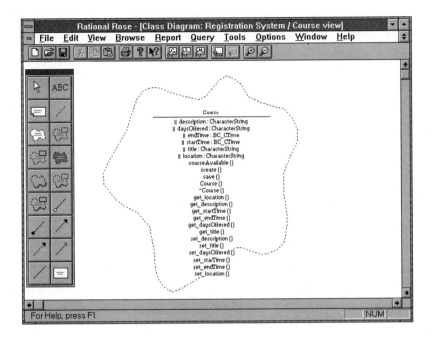

SUMMARY

THE MODEL MUST be updated to reflect any changes made while implementing the previous release. The reverse-engineering capability of Rose can be used to generate a model based on the current implementation, and this information can be merged with the original design model.

GLOSSARY

BASE PROJECT

A project that supplements the information in a program-specific project, usually with information about header files for compiler-specific libraries or other class libraries being used.

DESIGN MODEL

Model that reflects the current design of the system under development.

Chapter 15

Evolution: Team Development with Rational Rose

■

Parallel Development and Class Categories

■

Integration with Configuration-Management Systems

■

Summary

■

Glossary

PARALLEL DEVELOPMENT AND CLASS CATEGORIES

FOR THE MAJORITY of systems, a large number of classes are developed very quickly. Breaking up the model into individual units allows the model to be simultaneously manipulated by different teams of analysts, architects, and developers. The most effective way to break up the system is to use the concept of the class category (and its subcategories) as a unit of work. Good practice dictates that a unit should be "owned" by a single person. Since a category can be made up of nested categories, this strategy can be applied to the Rose model under creation.

Each category is an individual control unit, and the model is the sum of all the categories contained in it. Persistence is achieved by placing each unit in an individual file (.cat file). We have already seen how to create a control unit in Rose (Chapter 12); each category should be created as its own unit. The top-level diagram for the course registration problem follows.

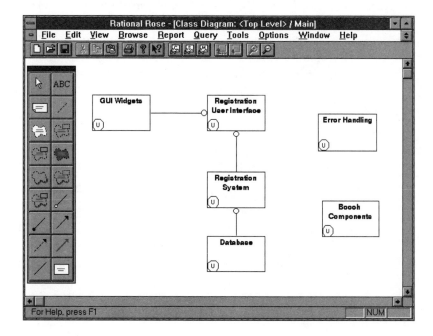

The adornment (symbol) for a control unit is a U in an octagon. The display can be turned off by choosing the Display/Unit Adornments command from the Options menu.

Making each category a separate unit means that the whole model does not have to be loaded when the model is opened; thus a large model can be opened quickly. On opening a model, the user is asked if the subunits should be loaded. If the answer is no, then the unit will not be loaded until needed (when the category is opened by double-clicking on the category).

Each unit in the model can also be write-protected. This allows a user to view the classes in the category but not to change them.

WRITE-PROTECTING CATEGORIES IN RATIONAL ROSE
1. Click on the category to be write-protected.
2. Choose the Units/Write Protect < category name > option from the File menu.

When the write-protected category is opened, toolbars are not displayed on any of the diagrams. Furthermore, when a class is opened, the < New > option for attributes and operations is not available. Thus, an analyst or designer may view the classes in the category but not change the category. Note that the title bar in the following screen illustrations on page 155 includes a "read-only" notice. Rose will automatically write-protect a control unit if the unit's access control in the platform file system is read-only.

INTEGRATION WITH CONFIGURATION-MANAGEMENT SYSTEMS

IN ORDER TO facilitate true multiuser management of the model units, each category file is placed under configuration-management (CM) control. Rose menu selections may be customized to add CM menu selections such as Check In, Check Out, Accept Changes, and Control. This is accomplished by creating a menu specification file that Rose reads at startup.

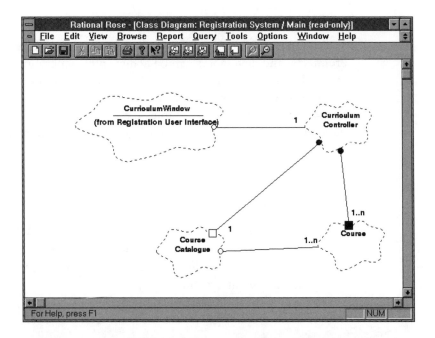

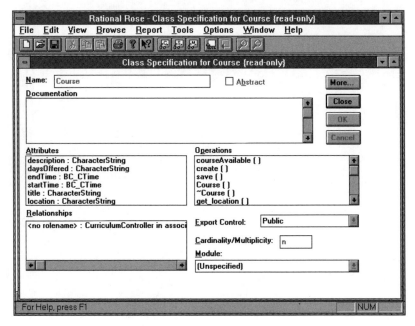

SUMMARY

SIMULTANEOUS MANIPULATION OF a model by teams of analysts, architects, and developers can be achieved by separating a model into individual control units. The ability to control individual units, coupled with Rose's ability to integrate with commercial configuration-management systems, enables team members to synchronize parallel activities and maintain multiple versions of their controlled units.

GLOSSARY

CONTROL UNIT

A unit, such as a category or subsystem, that can be loaded or saved independently and integrated into a configuration-management system.

Chapter 16

Overview of the OMT Method

■

The Object Modeling Technique

■

Fundamentals of OMT

■

The OMT Process

■

OMT System Development Activities

■

OMT System Development Strategies

■

Summary

■

Glossary

THE OBJECT MODELING TECHNIQUE

ONE OF THE most popular object-oriented system development techniques today is the Object Modeling Technique (OMT). First described in detail in the 1991 book, *Object-Oriented Modeling and Design,*[1] the technique has proponents and practitioners around the world.[2] It continues to be successful in many application domains: telecommunication, aerospace, financial services, transportation, geographic imaging, CASE tools, compilers, office automation, and traditional IS applications, to name a few. It is primarily used by system and software developers supporting full life-cycle development, targeting object-oriented implementations.

As any system needs to evolve to be successful and vibrant, even a methodology has to evolve, and the OMT methodology is no exception. An especially open methodology, OMT has benefited from continuing work by many contributors. Based on experiences in the field and led by Dr. Jim Rumbaugh, OMT has incorporated the best techniques of other renowned methodologists, such as Grady Booch and Ivar Jacobsen. Recommendations of practicing consultants, such as those from the Advanced Concepts Center of Lockheed Martin and the Rational Software Corporation have also played an important part in the ongoing development of OMT.

Because of its simple core notation, OMT has proven easy to understand, to draw, and to use. All the fundamental object-oriented principles are directly and expressively supported in a way that also minimizes the difficulties for experienced non-object-oriented developers. Besides the core notation, specialty notations have evolved to meet the needs of specific application domains such as interrupt-driven, real-time systems.[3]

---

[1] Rumbaugh, Blaha, Premerlani, Eddy, Lorensen. *Object-Oriented Modeling and Design.* Prentice Hall, 1991.

[2] For example, the text has been translated into Portuguese, French, German, Korean, and Japanese.

[3] As an example, see Chonoles, Michael J. and Clint Gilliam. "Real-Time Object-Oriented System Design Using the Object Modeling Technique (OMT). *Journal of Object-Oriented Programming,* June 1995.

FUNDAMENTALS OF OMT

THE OMT METHODOLOGY has three fundamental models, each representing a different view of the system under consideration. The three
views (the object, dynamic, and functional models) allow developers
to emphasize distinct aspects of the system as the circumstances
direct. Associated with each model is a micro process that lays out
the steps necessary to develop the model.

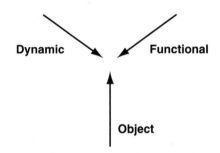

Dynamic   Functional

Object

Three model-based views of a system in the OMT Methodology
• Object model   Static structure
• Dynamic model   Control and behavior
• Functional model   Algorithms

The OMT Object Model

The OMT object model is the fundamental model on which the
remaining models are based. The object model captures the entities
that appear in the application and solution domain, their structure,
and the relationships among them. Class diagrams, showing the
existing classes and their relationships, along with an occasional
object diagram, showing the individual instances of classes, compose
the object model.

The OMT Dynamic Model

The OMT dynamic model indicates the dynamics of the objects and
their changes in state. By exploring the behavior of the objects over
time and the flow of control and events among the objects, the

dynamic model captures the essential behavior of the system. Scenarios are captured in message trace diagrams. These diagrams, along with state diagrams (sometimes called state charts), which show the life history of objects, compose the OMT dynamic model.

The OMT Functional Model

The OMT functional model captures algorithm requirements, design, and data flow. The functional model is best captured in textual form as a functional specification. In the early phases of system development, use cases capture the system's functional requirements. During later development phases, object message diagrams are used to capture design-level detail of the functional model.

Additional OMT Constructs

Besides the above-mentioned models, OMT has several additional constructs and diagrams that are often useful, though not part of any particular model. These can sometimes be considered part of several model views, depending on how they are emphasized in a particular project. Some of these are context diagrams, problem statements, and use cases. They are used to establish system boundaries, requirements, and to specify detailed behavior.

THE OMT PROCESS

OMT IS MORE than just a set of fundamental modeling entities and a coupled notation for drawing them. It is a full life-cycle process for understanding and developing systems, supporting contractual deliverables and measurables tied to acceptance criteria and metrics. But the OMT process cannot be a cookbook recipe. OMT is flexible enough to support creativity and to adapt to the realities of the development organization. The OMT process also supports the inevitable evolution of requirements that occur as a system develops. Because of its flexible and scalable, yet repeatable, process, OMT significantly contributes to efficient development of reliable, maintainable systems.

OMT SYSTEM DEVELOPMENT ACTIVITIES

THE OMT PROCESS can be best described as a set of stages or activities that need to be performed to construct a system. Each activity involves using multiple models and has several deliverables. For each activity, there is an associated macro process that describes the high-level approach to that activity. The following activities are typically identified:

> Conceptualization
>
> Object-oriented analysis
>
> Object-oriented design, comprising
>
>> System design
>>
>> Object design
>
> Implementation
>
> Testing and integration
>
> Deployment

Though the activities have a natural order, as indicated, when they are performed there is a considerable amount of overlap and iteration. For convenience, they are often represented in a linear fashion. The activities can be performed in several different orders as well as simultaneously, depending on the needs of the project at hand.

Conceptualization

Before one starts a project, there must be an idea for it. Conceptualization is the process of coming up with an idea for a system along with a general feel for its requirements and form. For that idea to be a good one, it must attempt to satisfy some business needs and goals, be grounded in technological and sociological feasibility, and include at least some of the ways the system will be used. To generate these good ideas, conceptualization often includes brainstorming, cost-benefit analysis, trade-studies, use-case analysis, and prototyping. The conceptualization step usually involves performing some high-level analysis and design steps in order to understand and delimit the possible solution. Depending on the scale of the project, conceptualization may be done formally or informally. By performing conceptualization at successive levels of detail, enough specifics of the desired system can be identified for formal analysis to begin.

Analysis

Analysis starts with the outputs of conceptualization (e.g., problem statement, requirements, use cases) and builds a model of the system from an external point of view. Besides the domain objects, which carry the real-world semantics, application objects are identified to capture the computer aspects of the application that are visible to the users. The outputs of analysis become the requirements for the system.

Object-Oriented Design

Object-oriented design encompasses all the efforts to design solutions to the analysis problem. These include the global, policy, and strategic architectural decisions made during system design and the more local, tactical decisions made during object design. Object-oriented design starts with making those decisions that affect the majority of the development and ends when the remaining open areas only affect the internal aspects of individual objects.

System Design

During system design, a high-level strategy for solving the problem is devised. Architectural styles and frameworks are chosen, general policy decisions are made, and the system's architectural skeleton is finalized. Depending on its size, the system is decomposed into smaller, more manageable components, and implementation approaches (e.g., software, hardware, operational procedures, database) are chosen for each component. During system design, the deployment releases are defined and planned.

Object Design

Object design elaborates upon the analysis models by adding increasingly more detail and by expanding high-level operations into lower-level operations. Each aspect (e.g., attributes, operations, associations, instances, inheritance) of a class is considered in detail. Algorithms and data structures are determined. Building upon the architectural frameworks chosen in system design, the object designer strives to meet the goals of efficiency, robustness, encapsulation, and reuse. Common patterns of responsibilities and communications are recognized and used as guides in designing and defining in detail the sets of interacting objects that comprise the system.

Implementation

During implementation, the designed objects are mapped directly into a realization technique. There may be many mappings (e.g., computer languages, databases, hardware devices, operational procedures). Decisions made at this point should only be of local scope; all global decisions should have been made in earlier design stages.

Testing and Integration

The implemented system must be validated against the requirements, so that defects can be identified and fixed, and the results validated. Cooperating objects are assembled, integrated, and tested as higher-level objects or subsystems until the whole system is integrated. Scenario- or use-case-based testing is also performed to verify functional requirements.

Deployment

After being validated, the system is released and installed or shipped to the field, installed, tested, and deployed at the customer site. Any additional bugs are noted and improvements suggested. The necessary maintenance is applied, and coordination with on-going releases continues.

As user requirements inexorably expand and as understanding of the system matures, new releases and versions are often needed. By supporting incremental and recursive development, OMT successfully encourages system evolution rather than system rewrite and rework.

OMT SYSTEM DEVELOPMENT STRATEGIES

A PERFECT SYSTEM architecture does not arise in complete form from the mind of the system architect, nor does a perfect system implementation arise from the hands of the developers. True system development is an evolutionary process that evolves in parallel with the understanding of the needs of the system and the practicalities of construction. Indeed, not only does understanding of the target improve as development continues, but the target itself is moving, because fundamental system requirements often change during the development process.

There are several potential responses to handling the risk of developing an evolving system, and object-oriented techniques make them all more feasible. By providing a concise modeling approach that encourages abstraction, encapsulation, and fidelity to the real world, OMT promotes the following:

- **Better requirements analysis:** Because system needs and requirements are understood better and earlier, some rework caused by misunderstanding of requirements is avoided.

- **More robust analysis and design:** The scope of changes can be limited, so that modifications can be made more easily.

- **Shorter cycle time:** Because a shorter development cycle is possible, the target system will change less during each development cycle. A faster cycle allows for additional releases in the same time.

- **Iteration:** Object-oriented techniques encourage decoupling of the components' interface dependencies by encapsulation, and they encourage decoupling of release-based dependencies by information hiding, so that it becomes more feasible to develop components or capabilities incrementally.

Development Life Cycles

OMT is suited for use in many different development life cycles, depending on the needs of the system. "The actual development process requires judgment to choose among many possible paths. A methodology provides guidelines to help the developer make these choices, but it cannot and should not attempt to prescribe a single right path for all problems and all developers."[4]

---

[4] Rumbaugh, James. "OMT: The Development Process." *Journal of Object-Oriented Programming* (May 1995).

System development proceeds in a recursive and fractal manner, with emphasis on the activities needed to control the project's risk. Traditional life-cycle models (e.g., waterfall, spiral, fountain) each emphasize different primary modes of iteration. It is usually best to use a combined approach in which development may progress in several of the dimensions at the same time.

Incremental Development Strategy

OMT is very well suited to an incremental development strategy based on a skeleton approach. The system is started top-down, and only a few key objects are expanded in depth. These objects should be just the minimal skeleton of the system, having only enough infrastructure to act as a base for one use of the system. The goal is to get the entire system running, but only with representative capabilities. Additional capabilities can then be added to the skeleton incrementally as a new top-down wave is started to add new features, to increase functionality, or to improve maturity.

Onion-Skin Architecture

OMT systems tend to be built from inside-out, in a layered approach. The innermost layers are more self-contained and have no knowledge of the outer layers. They are also the layers that tend to be more fundamental and, therefore, less likely to change. The inner core tends to consist of those objects found in the domain, and it is surrounded by the application objects and views.

SETTING UP RATIONAL ROSE FOR OMT
1. Choose Default Notation from the Options menu.
2. Choose OMT.

The following figure on page 167 shows Rational Rose class diagram editor with OMT notation.

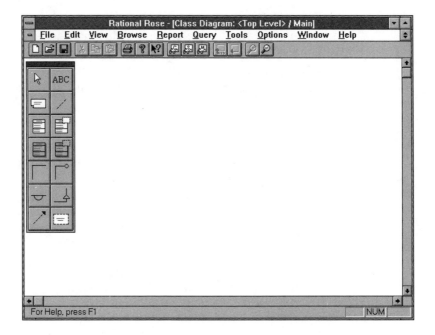

SUMMARY

OMT IS AN object-oriented methodology suitable for system and software development. It is based on three complementary views or models of the world—object, dynamic, and functional—and their associated notation. Additional diagrams and notation cross the models. The development of each model is governed by a micro process that lays out the low-level steps required to construct the model.

Systems are developed with OMT in a set of activities in which the models and diagrams serve as aids and tools, information repositories, and documentation. Each activity (conceptualization, analysis, system design, object design, implementation, testing, and deployment) is governed by a macro process that lays out the approach taken during that activity. OMT supports multiscale iteration, so that the development stages can be visited and revisited in different orders to reduce the risks in developing a system. In particular, OMT systems are usually developed using highly iterative approaches such as incremental delivery, skeleton approaches, or onion-skin architectures.

The OMT methodology is not a cookbook recipe. The basic ingredients, the models, notation, and diagrams are all there. The basic procedures and techniques, the stages, and their macro processes and micro processes are all defined, but the assembly and ordering of the steps are still under the creative control of the master chef.

GLOSSARY

CONCEPTUALIZATION

The process of coming up with an idea for a system, including a general idea of its requirements and form.[5]

DEPLOYMENT

The process of delivering, installing, testing, and maintaining new systems and releases of systems.

DYNAMIC MODEL

A description of the behavioral aspects of a system that identifies control, the sequencing and timing of operations, and changes in state of participating objects.

FUNCTIONAL MODEL

A description of the algorithmic and transformational aspects of a system that identifies functions and algorithms, mappings, constraints, and functional dependencies among participating objects and their behaviors.

IMPLEMENTATION

The specification of a particular mapping of the object design into a specific mix of realization techniques, such as software languages, database, hardware, operational procedure, and so on.

---

[5] *Object-Oriented Analysis (with OMT)*. Lockheed Martin Advanced Concepts Center, 1995.

MACRO PROCESS

The high-level approach to a development phase (e.g., analysis, object design), crossing all the models.

MICRO PROCESS

The series of low-level steps to follow when building a specific model.

OBJECT DESIGN

The elaboration of analysis models based on the frameworks, architectures, and strategies chosen during system design.

OBJECT MODEL

A description of the static aspects of a system that identifies the structure of the participating objects, including their relationships to other objects, attributes, and operations.

OBJECT-ORIENTED ANALYSIS

The application of an object-oriented methodology in order to understand, develop, and communicate system requirements and the *what* for the application domain.[6]

OBJECT-ORIENTED DESIGN

The application of an object-oriented methodology in order to understand, develop, and communicate the architecture and the details of how to implement requirements.[7]

OBJECT-ORIENTED METHODOLOGY

A development approach that organizes a system as a collection of objects that contain both data structure and behavior.[8]

---

[6] Ibid.

[7] Ibid.

[8] Ibid.

SKELETON APPROACH

An iterative development strategy in which a minimal infrastructure (the backbone) is implemented first, followed by some core application functionality. Each iteration adds more layers of the infrastructure and fleshes out the system with additional functionality.

SYSTEM DESIGN

The determination of the architectures, high-level structures, and global policies for a system.

Conceptualization: Defining the Need

■

High-Level Domain Analysis

■

Identifying the Actors

■

High-Level Use-Case Analysis

■

Context Diagram

■

Operations Concepts

■

Problem Statement

■

ESU Course Registration Problem Statement

■

Summary

■

Glossary

HIGH-LEVEL DOMAIN ANALYSIS

BECAUSE IT HAS been determined earlier in conceptualization that improving the ESU course registration system is worth considering, we should perform a high-level domain analysis of the current system. Since the conceptualization process is informal in this case study, the analysis identifies only the major fundamental domain classes of objects in the system. A more formal or more detailed conceptualization would use the full analysis notation, but for now, we can represent the classes as named rectangular boxes. This brief analysis revealed four classes: students, courses, professors, and the registration system itself. The remaining classes found in the ESU background problem statement are either not significant at this level, or they are views of other objects, or they can be considered designable parts (implementation objects) of the registration system.

DEFINING CLASSES IN RATIONAL ROSE
1. Choose New from the File menu option to create a new class diagram.
2. Select the class icon (rectangle) from the tool palette.
3. Click on the class diagram to draw the rectangle.
4. Type the name of the class inside the rectangle.

The high-level domain classes found in the ESU course registration system are shown in the following class diagram on page 174.

IDENTIFYING THE ACTORS

USE-CASE ANALYSIS is often started during the conceptualization activity, in order to identify the actors that interact with the system. An actor is a role played by a physical person or object when interfacing with the system. Typically, these actors are discovered in the

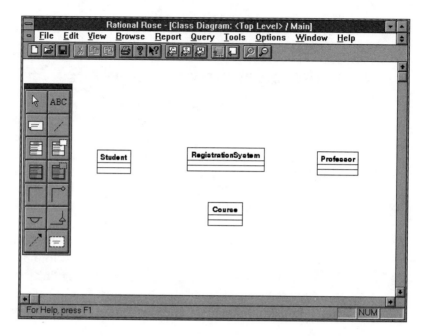

problem statement, by conversations with customers and domain experts, or by examining the outputs from previous levels of conceptualization.

For the ESU course registration problem, the following external actors have been identified: Student, Professor, Administrator, and University. The same individual may act in more than one role at different times, such as a professor who also takes courses, but the responsibilities of each role are different. At this level, the University is not a person.[1] It represents all the other external University systems that the course registration system needs to interact with, such as the billing system, and those that contain the current lists of students, professors, and courses. As more actors are discovered, they are added to the class diagram. Classes for additional actors have been added to the following class diagram.

---

[1] In a more realistic and detailed treatment of this problem, the individual components of the University actor would need to be identified.

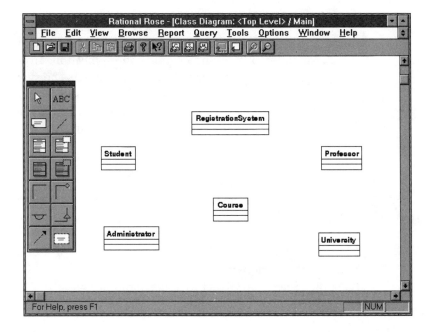

HIGH-LEVEL USE-CASE ANALYSIS

ONCE THE ACTORS have been determined, it is useful to come up with a rough cut for the use cases associated with them. For the purposes of an informal conceptualization phase, a use case describes an actor's typical use of the system. An actor may engage in more than one typical use if the uses are separated in time or place. As with actors, we can identify use by researching the domain, typically by interviewing the current and potential users.

The following table shows the fundamental communications for the Register for Courses use case.

ACTOR	USE CASE	FUNDAMENTAL COMMUNICATION
Student	Register for Courses	Identify self as student.
		Receive course information.
		Receive course-professor status.
		Request course selection.

CONTEXT DIAGRAM

WITH THE DEFINITION of the major objects and actors, and the determination of the fundamental communications from and to the actors, the system scope has been outlined. The system scope, or context, is a boundary separating the objects that need to be developed as part of the system, and what remains on the outside. The system scope is captured in a context diagram.

CREATING CONTEXT DIAGRAMS IN RATIONAL ROSE

1. Choose Scenario Diagram from the Browse menu option.
2. Double-click on < New > to display the New Scenario window.
3. Type Context Diagram in the Title field of the New Scenario window.
4. Select the Object Message radio button.
5. Click the OK button.

The following figure shows the New Scenario window.

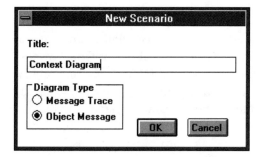

CREATING THE SYSTEM OBJECT AND
ACTOR OBJECTS IN RATIONAL ROSE

1. Select the object icon (rectangle) from the tool palette.
2. Click on the diagram window.
3. Type the name of the system in the cloud.
4. Repeat the steps above for each actor.

5. Select the link icon (line) from the tool palette, click on the object representing the system, and drag the link to an object representing an actor.
6. Repeat step 5 for each actor.
7. To create inputs to and outputs from the system, select the message icon (arrow) and click on the link between the actor and the system.
8. Type the names of the inputs and outputs on the message arrows.

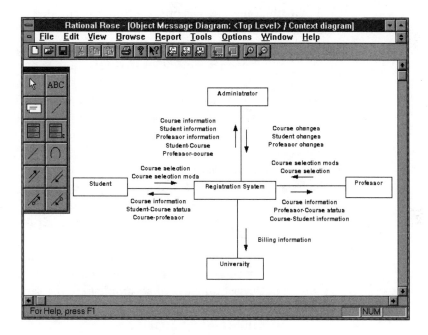

OPERATIONS CONCEPTS

TO CONTINUE DEVELOPING such a system any further, we need a more complete idea of how it will work. For example, the context diagram could be true of the existing paper/mainframe system as well as many possible, more automated systems. Though it is important to keep the possibilities open, you also need to get a picture, a *concept*, of how the system will actually work.

The operations concepts capture a description of how the system will be used, to distinguish it from other potential system solutions. It often contains a description of the target market—the subsets of actors that would want to (or could) use the system and the prerequisite hardware and software. The focus should be on particular system configurations, which allows a detailed vision of the new system to emerge. Besides the general system's operations concepts, we also need a general description of the approach and the frequency of each use case or fundamental communication.

Several operations concepts alternatives are chosen and evaluated by techniques such as brainstorming, facilitated discussions, research, and proof-of-concept prototyping. The costs of each potential solution are then compared to how well each solution meets the business requirements. This helps to determine the approaches to use in the system.

For example, the Student Registration use case can be done by paper forms, as it is typically done now, but there are other possibilities. Before we can progress much further, we need to know the essential outlines of this use case. Will it be done by paper forms, special punch cards, hard-wired terminals, dial-up computers, or a phone/keypad interface and IVR (interactive voice response)?[2] Similarly, the Student's fundamental communication of *identity*, currently sent by a combination social-security number and handwritten signature, may be sent by user ID and password, or by swiping a student ID card through a magnetic card reader attached to a terminal. It is not necessary to pick only one operations concept; most systems require several ways of accomplishing the same task, at least for backup contingency reasons. Some potential approaches should be scheduled for future releases.

Bounds and ranges on the frequency and performance requirements for the use cases and fundamental communications must also be determined. At this time we need only to understand the order of magnitude of the requirements. For example, will only one student be able to register at a given time, or will many students be able to

---

[2] For example, the 40,000 students at the University of Quebec at Montreal use their phones to complete their registration process. See "University Uses Off-the-Shelf CT-Resources to Upgrade Homegown Automated Student Registration." *Computer Telephony*, June 1995.

use the system simultaneously? How many students should the system be sized for, concurrently and in total—hundreds, thousands? Do we need to size the system for just this university, or do we plan to market the finished system to other universities? In the latter case, we should be sure that our system can handle the largest of universities (approximately 50,000 students).

PROBLEM STATEMENT

AFTER THE OPERATIONS concepts for each use case and fundamental communication are determined, they are summarized into a concise consistent statement describing the system that must be built. This problem statement incorporates any additional domain information that is available, and it is usually written in narrative paragraph form. In some situations, numbered requirements may be necessary to augment the narrative.

ESU COURSE REGISTRATION
PROBLEM STATEMENT

AT THE BEGINNING of each semester, the ESU Registrar's Office will provide a list of courses to students through a new on-line registration system. Information about each course, such as professor, department, and prerequisites, will be included to help students to make informed decisions.

The new system will allow students to review available courses and select four of them for the coming semester. In addition, each student will indicate two alternative choices in case a course becomes filled or canceled. No course will have more than ten students. No course will have fewer than three students. If a course has fewer than three students, it will be canceled. If there is enough interest in a course, than a second section will be established.

Professors must be able to access the on-line system to indicate which courses they will be teaching. They will also need to see which students have signed up for their courses.

The registration process will go on for three days. The first day will be for freshman orientation and registration. All other students will arrive on the second day of the semester to register. The third day will be used to resolve any outstanding course-assignment conflicts.

Once the course registration process is completed for a student, the registration system sends information to the billing system so the student can be billed for the semester.

As a semester progresses, students must be able to access the on-line system to add or drop courses.

The university prides itself on academic achievement in the Humanities. Most of the professors, administrators, and students are computer illiterate. Thus this system, unlike the old one, must be easy to use for all concerned.

SUMMARY

OMT'S APPROACH TO object-oriented conceptualization is an iterative approach that produces the inputs for object-oriented analysis. Customers, clients, users, and other stakeholders bring good ideas to conceptualization and offer the possibility of early and enthusiastic buy-in. During object-oriented conceptualization, the key domain objects and actors are identified and placed in context. The high-level use cases in which the actors participate are identified, and the fundamental communications that make up these use cases are also determined.

GLOSSARY

ACTOR

A person, object, or system that plays a defined role as it interfaces with the system under consideration.

BUSINESS GOALS

Prioritized statements of the organization's needs used to guide decision making and tradeoff throughout the development process.

CONTEXT DIAGRAM
> A graphical way to illustrate the boundaries of a system
> along with inputs and outputs to and from the system.

FUNDAMENTAL COMMUNICATION
> Those communications between an actor and the system
> that appear in the domain and are not dependent on any
> design. They are typically structural in nature; for example,
> they may involve identification, selection, or definition.

HIGH-LEVEL USE CASE
> An actor's typical use of a system for a particular purpose.

PROBLEM STATEMENT
> A narrative description of the system to be developed. It
> often includes numbered requirements and use cases.

STAKEHOLDERS
> The stakeholders of a system are those individuals and
> organizations that have a stake in the operation of the sys-
> tem. These can include such diverse groups as management,
> employees, shareholders, subcontractors, operators, users,
> regulatory and standards groups, consumers, and affected
> neighbors.

Chapter 18

Domain Analysis: Finding Classes

DOMAIN MODELS

ONCE THE CONTEXT of a system has been defined and the approach has been determined, it is possible to work further on the domain analysis models. We already have a high-level domain model from conceptualization that can now be fleshed out with more detail. Look for those classes that are natural to the domain and would be part of any solution to the problem. As applications and technology change—and they will—we can return to the domain models to see the fundamentals. The domain models have significant potential for reuse, not only within an organization, but throughout the industry. For example, all universities would have very similar domain models for their course registration systems, though their solutions might be very different.

As a practical approach, it is typical to assume that the design objects identified during the conceptualization process are now part of the domain. By iteration, the project progresses, and the context of the problem becomes more refined.

FINDING CANDIDATE CLASSES

THE STANDARD OMT approach to finding the domain classes is to examine the problem statement for candidate classes. Typically, nouns, pronouns, noun phrases, and implied nouns are underlined for further evaluation. Though it is not necessary to underline each occurrence of the same noun, it is necessary to determine if the word is being used in the same manner each time.[1]

As part of the extended problem statement, any nouns from the context diagram and the use cases may be evaluated as potential additions to the candidate list. Since their purposes are different, we

---

[1] The process outlined here appears simplistic, and it certainly cannot be practiced without some modification for systems with large problem statements. However, no feasible substitute for judicious examination of the things in the domain as a way to identify candidate classes has yet been put forward.

should be especially careful to watch for objects that are called by different names in the different sources.

Not every noun is a good candidate class. Unsuitable nouns for candidate classes include the following kinds:

- Duplicates of other classes

- Attributes of classes

- Attribute values

- States of classes

- Events or times

- Operations, processes, or algorithms

- Constraints

- Associations or other relationships

- Attributes of associations

- Roles of associations

- Arguments of operations or events

- Design or implementation

- Irrelevant or filler words

Evaluate each candidate noun to determine whether to keep it as a class. If a noun appears to be vague or ill-defined, it needs additional attention and research to determine its real meaning. Categorize the remaining, filtered nouns and keep them for later use at the appropriate time. Place all the defined terms in a model dictionary, in which every model element is briefly described. Once candidate classes have been determined, the domain model started during the conceptualization phase is updated to include the new objects.

The filtered list of candidate classes obtained in the registration problem is shown below.

1. Administrator
2. Course
3. Curriculum
4. Professor

5. Registrar'sOffice
6. RegistrationSystem
7. Roster
8. Section
9. Student
10. University

Standard naming conventions should be adopted for each project. A commonly chosen standard for class names is the use of singular nouns, all with initial capitals and no blanks. Start enforcing the project's standards at this time.

The class diagram is updated to show the additional domain classes. The domain classes found in the ESU course registration problem are shown in the following class diagram.

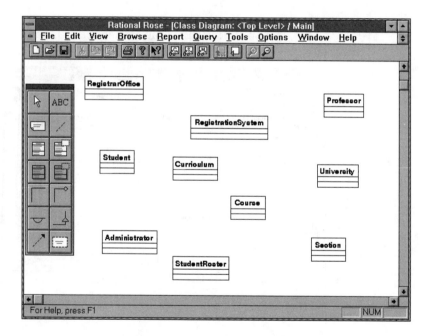

THE MODEL DICTIONARY

IN ADDITION TO the graphical depiction of a class, a semiformalized textual description is needed. Within Rational Rose for OMT, each class, like each model element (for example, attribute, operation, association) has an associated specification. The model dictionary is considered to be the sum of all the specifications in the system. Additional information about each class is included in its specification as development continues.

ADDING THE DEFINITION

TO THE CLASS SPECIFICATION

1. Double-click on the class box to display the Class Specification window.
2. Type the definition in the Documentation field.
3. Click the OK button.

The Class Specification for the Student class follows.

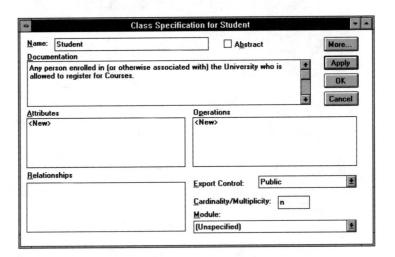

SUMMARY

DOMAIN MODELING IS performed to deepen the developers' understanding of the fundamental nature of the problem. Candidate classes are identified by investigating the entities in the problem statement and other outputs from conceptualization. This may be done by identifying the noun and nounlike phrases in the problem statement, use cases, and context diagrams. After filtering duplicated terms, attributes, and operations, we add the remaining domain classes to the domain model. Model dictionary entries are added for each kept domain class.

GLOSSARY

CANDIDATE CLASS

>A noun, pronoun, noun phrase, or implied noun that is being investigated as a potential class.

DOMAIN OBJECT (CLASS)

>An object (class) that is fundamental to the domain and is required in any possible description of the world it represents. In iterative development, objects (classes) added because of design considerations may be considered domain objects (classes) at the next iteration.

MODEL DICTIONARY

>Includes brief description (two or three sentences) of each model element within the system. Elements include classes, associations, attributes, types, operations, arguments, events, states, and any other named entity.

SPECIFICATION

>Additional information for each modeling entity (for example, class, association, attribute, operation). Includes model dictionary information.

Chapter 19

Domain Analysis: Capturing Associations

ASSOCIATIONS

BESIDES IDENTIFYING THE domain classes, we need to to identify the fundamental structural relationships among them. These relationships, called *associations* and *links*, are the glue that holds the models together.

A link is a bidirectional structural connection between two (or more) objects.[1] An association is a semantically similar group of links between objects that belong to the same endpoint classes. One might say that a link is an instance of an association in a manner similar to the way an object is an instance of a class.

As an example, let us analyze the relationships among three of the domain classes: Student, Course, and Section. By going back to the problem statement or the use cases, we see that "a Student *Registers For* a Course." Remembering that associations are bidirectional, you can also say that "a Course *Is Registered For By* a Student." This association was identified from the first use case, named Register for the actor Student. Often the essential purpose of a use case is to create or maintain an association.

Starting with the second Student use case, that of Add/Drop, analysis shows that the Student is actually Adding/Dropping assignments to Sections. Thus, the association might best be named "a Student *Is Assigned* a Section" or "a Section *Is Assigned* a Student."

There is also a recursive relationship among the instances of courses. That is, from our problem statement, we see that "a Course *Requires* Course," in the sense of prerequisites.

An association is drawn as a line between the associated classes. An association may be named if it makes the intent clearer, typically by using an active verb or verb phrase that conveys the meaning of the relationship. The name is usually written in italics and with initial capitals. Because the name of the association would often be read differently depending on which side is the start,

---

[1] It is possible to have links and associations connecting three or more objects. These ternary, or higher-order, associations are rare, and can usually be represented as multiple binary associations.

wherever possible we use a left-right or top-down convention to determine the preferred name.

CREATING ASSOCIATIONS IN RATIONAL ROSE

1. Select the association icon (straight line) from the tool palette.
2. Click on one of the associated classes.
3. Drag the association line to the other associated class.
4. If a reflexive association is needed (from a class to itself), while drawing the association, drag the line so that it bends, and then drop the association line. Then select the original class. The line will be drawn that completes the association.

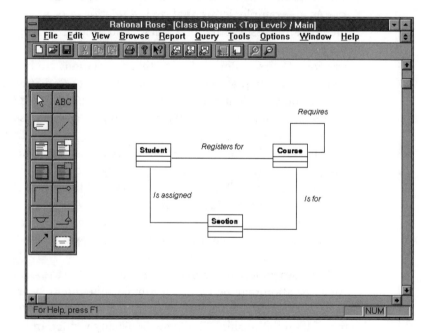

MULTIPLICITY AND ROLES

THE MULTIPLICITY OF an association is the number of instances that participate in the association. Just as an association has two ends, or *roles,* an association has two multiplicities, one at each end of the association. Some common multiplicity indicators are given in the following table.

Multiplicity Notation		
OMT Notation		Meaning
		unspecified (i.e., to be determined)
		to *exactly* 1
o		to *optional* (i.e., zero or 1)
•		to *many* (i.e., zero or more)
•	1–4	range of 1 through 4
•	1,4,5	1, or 4, or 5
•	1+	to more than 1 (i.e., zero or more)
•	1–5, 7,10+	range of 1 through 5, 7, and 10 or more

As analysis progresses and understanding becomes deeper, we can increase the specificity of the multiplicity. Typically, associations are first drawn as unadorned lines and then the multiplicity balls are added to distinguish the three major types of roles: to *1,* to *optional* (zero or 1), or to *many* (zero or more).

As more details are determined, the specific multiplicity numbers are added. Of course, if an explicit multiplicity is determined through domain analysis, or as a requirement, we can capture the multiplicity then. To make associations clearer, the roles (that is, the ends of the association) are often labeled with names that state how the instances on that end can be called. Role names are especially important when an association is recursive, that is, when it connects instances of the same class to each other. Role names may also be used to indicate the aspects of the class that are visible via the association.

To determine the multiplicity, examine each association and determine the multiplicity for each role, one at a time. Do the forward direction and then the reverse. Assign role names if they help clarify the association.

Determining multiplicity and roles during domain analysis helps define the classes and how they relate to each other. Try to capture the meaning of the terms as used by domain experts, and expect some disagreements. For example, in the given interpretation of the ESU course registration problem, a student is allowed to take no courses, and a course is allowed to have no sections. Other solutions are possible. Choose the dominant interpretation by the available experts as the one to be captured in the domain model for reference.

ADDING MULTIPLICITY AND ROLES IN RATIONAL ROSE
1. Double-click on the association or aggregation link.
2. Enter the multiplicity in the Cardinality/Multiplicity field of the Association Specification.
3. Type the role name in the Role field of the Association Specification.
4. Click on the OK Button.

AGGREGATION

THERE IS A stronger form of association, called aggregation, that shows the relationship of a whole to its parts. This type of association is very common, and it has been found useful to indicate it by a special adornment to the association line. A diamond is placed at the "whole" class to indicate that this association is an aggregation. Aggregations are not typically named; they are read using the words *has* or *contains*.

In the registration problem, an obvious aggregation is the relationship by which the Curriculum *contains* many Courses.

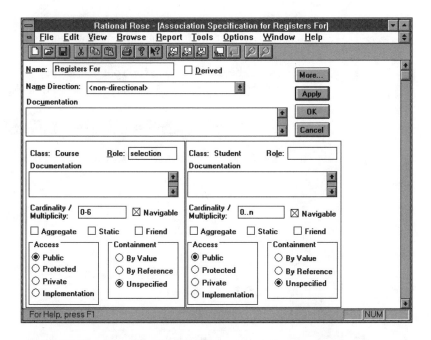

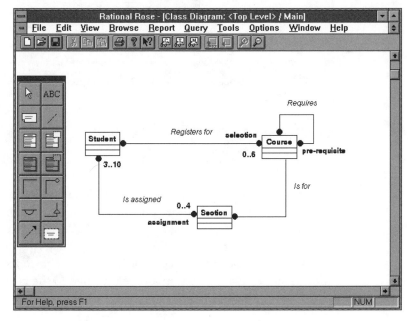

CREATING AGGREGATIONS IN RATIONAL ROSE

1. Select the aggregation icon (line with a diamond at one end) from the tool palette.
2. Click on the class playing the role of the "part" and drag the aggregation line to the class playing the role of the "whole."

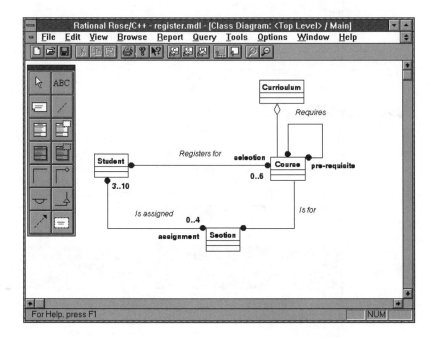

NOTES AND CONSTRAINTS

MOST SYSTEMS UNDER development involve a collection of assumptions and decisions that need to be documented. This information is contained in a note that may be attached to any of the elements in the model. Constraints are also documented in the same note format, but are enclosed in braces: {}. In the course registration problem, the reflexive *Requires* association needs additional specification, because a course cannot directly or indirectly require itself. This information is documented in a note attached to the class.[2]

---

[2] Most reflexive associations require additional elaboration to specify whether cycles are allowed and whether they are singularly rooted or multiply rooted (a tree or lattice structure).

DEFINING NOTES IN RATIONAL ROSE

1. Select the note icon (folded rectangle) from the tool palette.
2. Click on the diagram to draw the note.
3. Select the attachment icon (dashed line) from the tool palette.
4. Click on the note and drag the attachment line to the appropriate element.

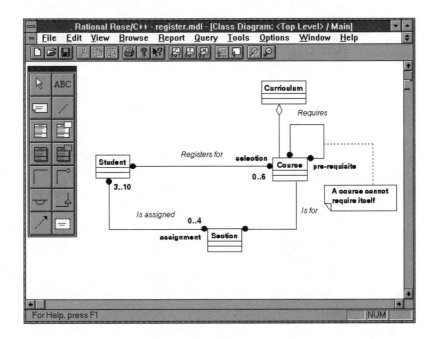

REMAINING DOMAIN ANALYSIS

TO COMPLETE THE domain analysis for the problem, we would continue the analysis until the object model for the entire problem domain was constructed. The fundamental operations on the domain objects are then identified, either from knowledge of the world, or by constructing life-cycle state diagrams *(dynamic model)* for those domain objects that have discernible state. The operations are described, and any required algorithms are captured *(functional model)*.

In the limited course registration problem as stated, there is not much need for a dynamic or functional domain model. The techniques to construct them will be explained later. However, if we were developing a complete, realistic course registration system, constructing the dynamic and functional models would be quite valuable. For example, the class Section has an interesting domain life cycle: it would be useful to model how new sections are made and canceled as students are assigned. The algorithm for how students are assigned to sections should also be investigated. For example, is it first-come, first-served? Is an optimization needed? Are there some preferences for seniors? Such algorithmic requirements need to be captured.

SUMMARY

DOMAIN ANALYSIS IS performed to deepen our understanding of the fundamental nature of the problem. The associations between the classes are found to determine the structural relationships appearing in the real world. Assigning multiplicity and role names to the roles of these associations more precisely captures the meaning of these relationships.

Associations are bidirectional relationships connecting two (or more) classes. Reflexive associations connect instances of the same class. Aggregations are a strong form of association that indicate the relationship of a whole to its parts.

GLOSSARY

AGGREGATION

A strong form of association that indicates the relationship of a whole to its parts.

ASSOCIATION

A family of links between objects of the same endpoint classes.

CONSTRAINT

A relationship between elements that limits their values.

LINK

A bidirectional structural relationship between one object and another.

MULTIPLICITY

The number of instances at one end of an association that link up with one instance at the other.

REFLEXIVE ASSOCIATION

An association that relates one object of a class to another object (or objects) of the same class.

ROLE

One end of an association. A role has an associated multiplicity and role name.

Chapter 20

Domain Analysis:
Attributes and Operations

CLASS FEATURES

PART OF THE process of identifying domain objects is capturing and defining their essential properties and behaviors. Such key features distinguish an object from others and further define the roles in which the objects participate. By indicating the objects' key responsibilities, analysts build an increasingly complete picture of how the domain works.

There are two types of features that need to be identified (in OMT)—attributes and operations. The difference between them can be found by considering a class in several ways. If we think of an object as maintaining an encapsulation of state, then attributes are abstractions of the state, and operations are the ways that the state can be changed. Another approach considers an object as a coherent bundle of responsibilities. In this approach both attributes and operations are really responsibilities: attributes are the things that the object is responsible to know, while operations are the behaviors that the object is responsible for performing.

ATTRIBUTES

AN ATTRIBUTE IS a property or characteristic of a class. Each object in a class has a value for every attribute defined for the class. Attributes should be pure values without individual identity and not objects themselves.[1]

Many of the attributes of a class are found in the problem statement or other conceptualization outputs, or they may be detected when creating the model dictionary for the class. Attributes also can be discovered by identifying those responsibilities of the class that are "things that this object knows." As we might expect, during domain analysis, domain knowledge can also add to the attributes for a class.

---

[1] For example, a student's address is an attribute. If two address values are the same, they are the same address. However, even if two students' attributes are all identical, they do not become the same student.

A definition for each attribute is added to the model dictionary. Attributes should generally have very little structure, but it is appropriate to have complex attributes, such as addresses, when they have domain meaning. During analysis, we use an attribute's data type to capture units or ranges when such information is needed for clarification. We specify the remaining information about type, such as length, precision, and format, as well as default values during design.

The following attributes can be defined for the course registration problem:

- Course—title, description, department, credit

- Section—startTime, endTime, daysOffered, location

- Student—name, address, phoneNumber, studentID, major, year

- Professor—name, address, phoneNumber, employeeID, department

Some of these attributes could benefit from some simple typing at this time; for example,

- credit : Hours

- location: BldgRoom

- year: (FRE,SOP,JUN,SEN,GRD,OTH)

Follow a style guide while defining attributes. In this case study, an attribute name starts with a lowercase letter. Attributes whose names are composed of multiple words are closed up and the first letter of each additional word is capitalized. During analysis, attribute names are simple nouns or noun phrases that identify the values the attribute holds. When data types are used to clarify the range or units, they usually start with an initial capital (as class names do). For enumerated types, just choose an appropriate data type name, or show values as all capitals, as in the last item in the list above. Default or initial values may also be used at this time if they clarify the attribute.

CREATING ATTRIBUTES IN RATIONAL ROSE

1. Display the Class Specification window by double-clicking on the class.
2. Double-click on < New > in the Attributes field.
3. Type the attribute name, data type, initial value, and documentation in their respective fields.
4. If additional attributes are desired for this class, select the Another button. Otherwise select the OK button.

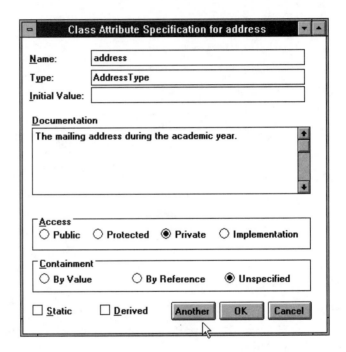

SHOWING ATTRIBUTES IN RATIONAL ROSE

1. Position the mouse pointer near the class and click the right mouse button.
2. Select the Edit Compartment option.
3. Select the attributes to be shown on the class diagram and click the > > button to move the selected items to the Show Items field.
4. Click the OK button.

The following diagram shows the attributes for some of the classes from the ESU course registration problem.

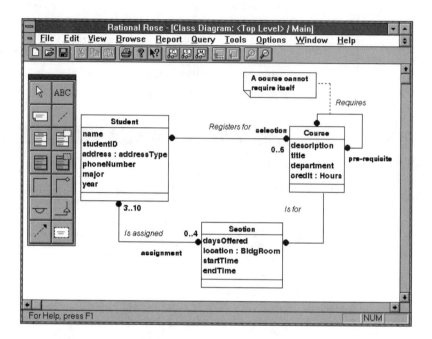

OPERATIONS

THE BEHAVIOR OF an object is described by the operations of the class. Such operations are the domain-specific changes in state that the object may endure or the behavior and responsibilities that it may be asked to perform. During domain analysis, the problem statement and other outputs from conceptualization are examined to determine potential operations.

Minor access operations used to *get* or *set* attributes or associations are not shown during domain analysis. All attributes identified for a class are assumed to have appropriate access operations. Likewise, creation, initializing, or destruction operations are not usually shown unless they have significant and interesting domain meaning.

For actors, the domain operations include those required for sending to the system the incoming events for which an actor is responsible. The actors are also responsible for receiving those events directed to them by the system.

As with attributes, follow your organization's style guide while defining operations. Generally, the same notation is used for attributes and operations. Though typically identified during design, operations may have arguments, argument types, and return types indicated. A sample of the full notation is as follows: operation(firstArg:ArgType,. . .): ReturnType

The following domain operations can be defined for the course registration problem:

- Course—offer(), cancel(), makeNewSection()

- Section—reschedule(), addStudent(), dropStudent()

- Student—enroll(), logon(), requestCatalog(),
  register(courseList), add(section), drop(section),
  receiveCatalog(), receiveAssignment()

CREATING OPERATIONS IN RATIONAL ROSE

1. Display the Class Specification window by double-clicking on the class.
2. Double-click on < New > in the Operations field to display the Operation Specification.
3. Add the operation name, return class, and documentation to the Name, Return Class, and Documentation fields in the Operation Specification.
4. If the operation requires arguments, double-click on the < New > field in the Arguments dialog box.
5. Type the name, type, and default value (if any) for the argument. If another argument is needed for the operation, select the Another button. When finished, select the OK button.
6. When back to the Operation Specification dialog, select the Another button if more operations are desired for this class; otherwise select the OK button.

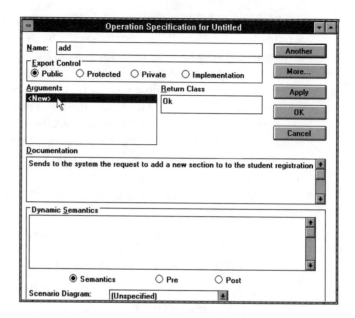

SHOWING OPERATIONS IN RATIONAL ROSE

1. Position the mouse pointer near the class and click the right mouse button.
2. Select the Edit Compartment option.
3. Select the operations to be shown on the class diagram and click the > > button to move the selected items to the Show Items field.
4. Click the OK button.

The class diagram follows on page 211.

DELETING ATTRIBUTES OR
OPERATIONS IN RATIONAL ROSE

1. Double-click on the class to bring up the Class Specification dialog.
2. Select the attribute (or operation) that you wish to delete.

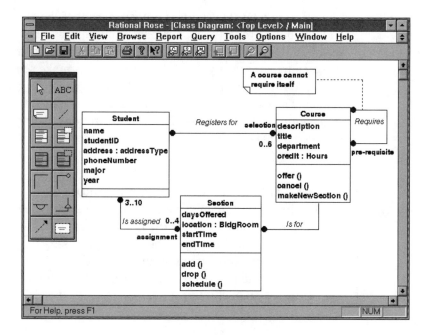

3. Press the delete key.
4. Select the Yes button on the Delete Attribute pop-up.
5. Select the OK button.

The following figure shows the Delete Attribute window.

LINK ATTRIBUTES

WE OFTEN IDENTIFY attributes that are naturally part of the domain, but that do not actually belong to any object. For example, a student might select six courses: four primary and two alternate courses.

The primary/alternate status is not a property of the class Student, and it is not a property of Course (or Section); it is a property of the selection. Only in the context of the association between a student and a course does the primary/alternate status make sense.

Link attributes are attributes that exist for each link of an association. They are drawn as unnamed classes that are attached to an association. If the link attributes have operations, they may be modeled as named classes attached to an association.

CREATING LINK ATTRIBUTES IN RATIONAL ROSE
1. Create an unnamed class and place it slightly lower than the association that needs the link attribute.
2. Add the attribute(s) to the unnamed class.
3. Select the link attribute (the "horse-collar" icon).
4. Select the newly created class and drag the link attribute to the relationship line.

The following class diagram on page 213 shows a link attribute.

QUALIFIERS

OCCASIONALLY LINK ATTRIBUTES are found that serve as names or keys in some context. OMT has the ability to indicate special attributes that are part of association and are used to select objects across the association. When a qualifier is used, the multiplicity of the association needs to be revisited, because typically only one object is selected for a given value of the qualifier.

Consider the Course class. In many universities, a course may be offered by several departments. Instead of modeling the department as an attribute of the course, the department is best modeled as a separate class that has a *Sponsors* association with the Course class. If each Department class uses a courseID to identify its courses, a Course may have more than one courseID, one for each sponsoring department. This is modeled as a qualifier. It is a name to identify

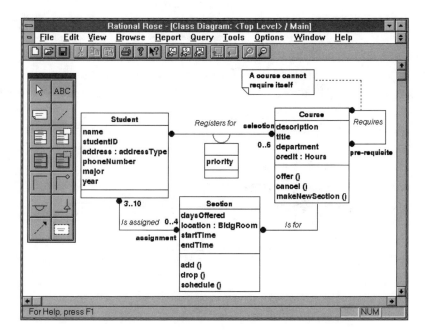

a Course from the perspective of a Department. In addition, if there is a requirement that a Course may be selected by its courseID, we can use a qualifier to capture the selection requirement.

CREATING QUALIFIERS IN RATIONAL ROSE

1. Display the Association Specification window by double-clicking on the association line.
2. Click the More button.
3. Choose the New Key/Qualifier option. Enter the qualifier name and, if desired, its type and documentation.
4. Click the OK button.
5. Select the other end of the association (the other role) and update the multiplicity if necessary.

Qualifiers are shown in the following diagram.

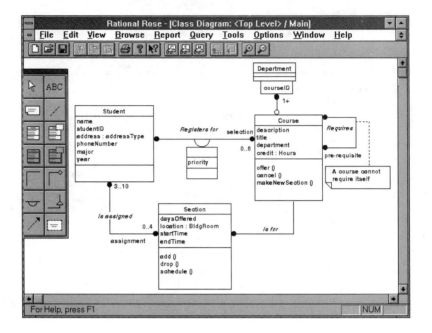

SUMMARY

AS DOMAIN ANALYSIS continues, the attributes and operations that are discernible from the domain and those found as a result of conceptualization are added to the models. Attributes are properties of a class, and each instance of a class has its own values for the attributes.

Operations are behaviors that an object performs or transformations that an object undergoes. During domain analysis, units and ranges are indicated for attributes and arguments if they clarify their purpose.

Link attributes are placed on associations to indicate special attributes that are not properly part of any object but are part of the association. Qualifiers are special link attributes that are used to name or select objects across an association.

GLOSSARY

ATTRIBUTE

> A named property of a class.

ACCESS OPERATION

> A low-level operation that just gets or sets an attribute or an association.

LINK ATTRIBUTE

> An attribute that does not belong to either role, but applies to the association.

OPERATION

> A transformation that an object undergoes or a behavior that an object performs.

QUALIFIER

> A special link attribute that is used to name, select, or qualify particular instances participating in an association.

Chapter 21

Domain Analysis: State Modeling

- Life-Cycle Modeling

- Sample University Object Life Cycle

- State Definitions

- System States

- Substates

- Summary

- Glossary

LIFE-CYCLE MODELING

DURING DOMAIN ANALYSIS, the fundamental life-cycle histories of the classes also need to be analyzed and captured. By understanding the life cycles and state changes of an object, the analysts can begin to understand how the objects interact, and the order in which they interact. Analysts construct a state transition diagram for each object with interesting behavior, and for strongly coupled aggregates.

Each state transition diagram identifies all the states of a single object, as well as the events or messages that cause a transition of that object from one state to another. At this time, the state transition diagrams may also show the events and messages that the object is sensitive to in each state.

For each received event, the diagram shows the action that the object takes upon receiving that event. For each state, the activities that the object performs while waiting for the next event are also captured.

Normally an object only makes a transition to a new state upon receiving an event; however, analysis can reveal automatic transitions that are caused by the completion of some internal activity.

SAMPLE UNIVERSITY OBJECT LIFE CYCLE

THE SECTION OBJECT has an interesting life cycle. It is created when the Course determines that there is enough demand for it. Students are assigned to the Section as a result of their requests. Once three students are assigned to a Section, it is considered an officially offered Section; when ten students have been assigned, then it must be closed and the Course notified not to assign any more students. After registration ends, any Section with less than three students is canceled, and Sections can now receive add and drop requests. If all the students drop the Section, it is canceled; otherwise, it remains until archived. If enrollment reaches ten students, no new add requests are accepted.

The following states have been identified:

■ *Proposed Section*—Less than three students

■ *Offered Section*—During Registration, a Section with more than three students

■ *Closed Offered Section*—During Registration, a Section with ten students

■ *Open Section*—A Section being taught with less than ten students

■ *Closed Section*—A Section being taught with exactly ten students.

Note that often a state may be defined as a partition of the possible values of an object. In this case, the states of a Section are primarily defined using ranges of the number of students.

CREATING STATE TRANSITION
DIAGRAMS IN RATIONAL ROSE

1. Click to select the class that needs a state transition diagram.
2. Select State Diagram from the Browse menu.
3. The State Diagram window is opened.
4. Select the state icon (rounded rectangle) from the tool palette.
5. Click on the state transition diagram to draw the state.
6. Repeat steps 4 and 5 to draw additional states.

Check for initial and final states of an object. Knowing the conditions that cause an object to come into being or to be destroyed helps the developer to understand the essence of the object. For the Section object there is one initial state (with ● on the diagram) and two final states (with ●s)—one caused by canceling a course and one caused by archiving the course.

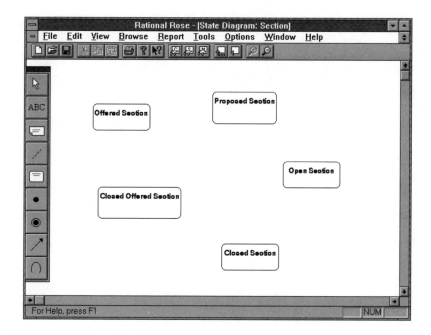

- *Startup*—Creation of section

- *Canceled*—Either not enough students to open a section or all students dropped during the semester

- *Archived*—A section held to completion and off-lined

ADDING INITIAL AND FINAL STATES IN RATIONAL ROSE
1. Select the initial state icon (•) from the tool palette.
2. Click on the state transition diagram to draw the initial state icon.
3. Select the final state icon (◉) from the tool palette.
4. Click on the state transition diagram to draw the final state icon.
5. Repeat step 4 to create additional final state icons.

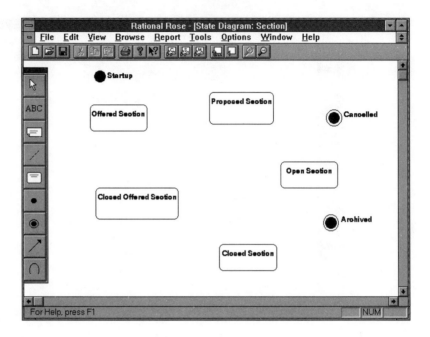

STATE DEFINITIONS

STATES ARE TYPICALLY defined by a textual description and a set of range constraints on the object's (or related object's) attribute values. As each state is defined, we capture the information in the model.

ADDING THE STATE DEFINITION IN RATIONAL ROSE
1. Double-click on the state of interest to make the State Specification window visible.
2. Type the state description in the Documentation text box.
3. Click the OK button.

The State Specification window for the Offered Section state follows on page 223.

Certain states actively enforce range constraints. These constraints may be added to the state transition diagram.

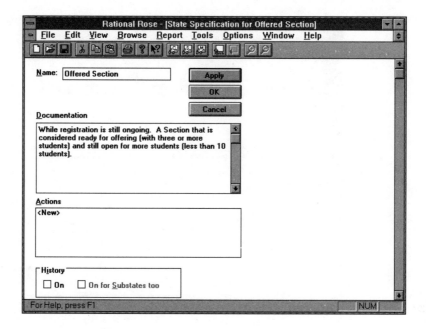

ADDING CONSTRAINTS TO STATES IN RATIONAL ROSE

1. Double-click on the state of interest to make the State Specification window visible.
2. Double-click on < New > to make the State Action window visible.
3. Select the Action and Entry until Exit radio buttons for Type and When.
4. Enter the constraint in the Action field.
5. Click the OK button.

The State Transition diagram showing constraints follows on page 224.

Transitions are the changes in state and are drawn by directed arrows from the initial state to a target state. Attached to each transition is the causing event or the condition that must be satisfied for the transition to fire. In association with a transition, an object can notify another object or perform some action of its own. An object does not always transition when an event arrives. It may just

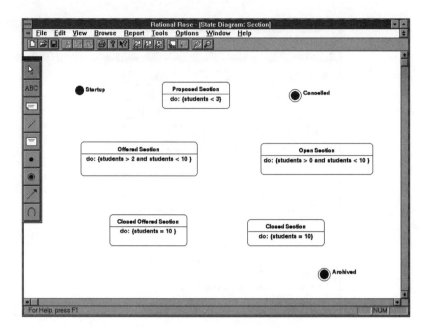

undergo a self-transition, that is, reenter its own state or take some internal action.

DEFINING TRANSITIONS IN RATIONAL ROSE

1. Choose the arrow from the tool palette.
2. Place the selection point on the initial state in the transition and drag to the target state in the transition. This creates an unlabeled transition.
3. Double-click on a selected transition to bring up the State Transition Specification for the transition.
4. Type the triggering event in the Event text box. If a condition must be satisfied for the transition to fire, type the condition in the Condition text box.
5. If there is some action that is associated with the transition, type the action in the Action text box.
6. If another object must be notified of this transition, indicate the target object in the Send Target text box and the event being sent in the Send Event text box.

7. Document the transition in the Documentation box.
8. Select the OK button when done.

The updated State Transition diagram follows.

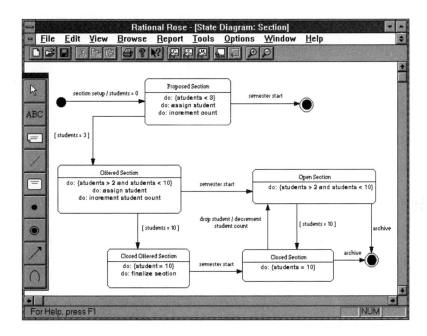

SYSTEM STATES

ANOTHER TASK DURING domain analysis is the capturing of any system-level states or modes. By looking at the problem statement and other outputs from conceptualization, the analyst can detect events or times that change the fundamental behavior of the system. The registration system has a relatively simple life cycle that can be determined from the problem statement and some domain knowledge.

1. *Preregistration*—Administrator sets up system
2. *Registration*—Ongoing registration
3. *In semester*—Classes being taught

4.   *Historical*—On-line, but no changes allowed
5.   *Archived*—Off line

SUBSTATES

THE STATE TRANSITION chart notation allows for substates, that is, for life cycles within a state. All the transitions and internal actions that the superstate is subject to also apply to all the substates. Substates not only simplify the diagram by reducing the number of independent states that need to be identified, but they support the iterative process of step-wise refinement with encapsulation and information hiding. They also allow us to defer investigation and definition of internal activities until later during development.

1.   *Registration.Day1* Freshman registration
2.   *Registration.Day2* Registration for all
3.   *Registration.Day3* Conflict resolution
4.   *In Semester.ChangesAllowed* Processes Add/Drops
5.   *In Semester.Closed* After cut-off date, special administrative changes only

It is also possible to have superstates that generalize previously existing substates. Because several responses to events are the same when in the *Registration* and in the *In Semester* states, it is possible to make them part of a new superstate, *Active*.

CREATING SUBSTATES AND
SUPERSTATES IN RATIONAL ROSE
1.   Create a new state as previously discussed by selecting the state icon from the tool palette.
2.   Place the new state inside the state you wish to divide. It may be necessary to resize the states by dragging on their handles.
3.   Create transitions in the same manner as before, by selecting the transition icon from the palette and drawing the transition line from the initial state to the target state.

4. A state's substates may be hidden by selecting a state and choosing Hide Substates from the View menu. The contained substates will not be shown, but a small ★ will appear in the lower right corner of the state. Deselecting Hide Substates will uncover the hidden states at the current level.

5. To create superstates, create a new state on the diagram and drag the existing states to place them in the new state. The superstate will resize to accommodate the new substates.

6. Rose allows the user to create transitions directly to states that are hidden. To do so, draw a transition from the initial state to the superstate of the hidden state.

7. Double-click on the transition to bring up the State Transition Specification.

8. Hidden substates may be chosen from the two pull-down menus From or To in the Transition Between Substates field. A transition to a hidden substate shows as a stubbed transition line ending inside the superstate.

The completed state diagram for the system follows on page 228.

SUMMARY

DOMAIN ANALYSIS CONTINUES to capture details of the domain by constructing state transition diagrams. The study of the life cycles of significant objects and aggregates with interesting behavior yields a better understanding of the fundamentals of the domain and the system. The system's states, or modes, are also captured by treating the system as a whole as an object.

The state transition diagrams capture the initial, final, and all intermediate states of an object, and the events that cause the transitions between them. When an object is in a particular state, that is, when its attribute values are within the state's defining attribute ranges, it always has the same qualitative response to incoming events and messages.

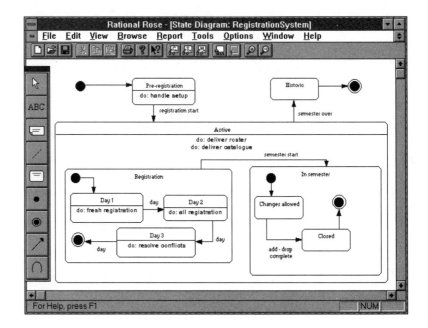

In response to an event, an object can perform an instantaneous action and or transition to another state. When in a state, an object can perform activities while waiting for other events. Substates can be defined within a state.

GLOSSARY

ACTION

> An object's response to an event. An action is considered to take no time at the current scale and cannot be interrupted.

ACTIVITY

> The behavior that an object performs while in a state and waiting for an event. An activity takes time at the current scale and may be interrupted by an event.

AUTOMATIC TRANSITION
> A transition that occurs automatically after the activity within the originating state is completed.

EVENT
> An instantaneous occurrence relevant to a receptive object.

GUARD CONDITION
> A logical condition that must be true before an object can respond to an incoming event or perform an automatic transition.

STATE
> One of a finite number of characteristic conditions of an object, during which the pattern of the object's response to events is qualitatively the same.

STATE TRANSITION DIAGRAM
> A diagram that shows the possible states of a given class, the events that cause transition from one state to another, and any resulting actions or activities.

SUBSTATE
> A partition of a state that refines the state definition and inherits some behavior from the state.

SUPERSTATE
> A state that contains substates.

TRANSITION
> A change in state.

Chapter 22

Application Analysis

APPLICATION ANALYSIS

DOMAIN ANALYSIS MODELS the fundamentals of the world, while application analysis models the fundamentals of the system to be built. It is now necessary to consider those entities (e.g., objects, associations) that, while not necessary parts of the world, are necessary and visible parts of the system. First, we captured the requirements of any system in this domain; now we need to capture the requirements of this particular system, with its design approach from conceptualization.

Application analysis uses modeling techniques similar to those performed in domain analysis (object, dynamic, and functional modeling), but now it includes those classes that represent the interface between the application system and the user. These application objects need to be explored to determine the full scope and requirements of the system to be built and to determine the development and release schedule, using the terminology that the users and clients would use. Thus we model the requirements, the visible and testable features of the system.

Objects that are part of the domain but are not application objects and need no further development are still identified, but they are set aside for later consideration.

APPLICATION OBJECTS

APPLICATION ANALYSIS CONSIDERS, for example, the following classes that are not typically found in the domain, but are part of (or should be considered part of) the application's requirements.

- *Controllers*—Control and sequence behavior, systems, applications, or user interfaces

- *Surrogates*—Represent system knowledge of external objects

- *View/Presentations*—Present domain objects to users, screens, displays, reports

- *Devices*—Represent physical devices in the system

- *Interfaces*—Translate information from one system to another, crossing media boundaries

Two other categories of objects that are sometimes added during application analysis are the following:

- *Reifications*—Represent functions, events, or data that need to be logged, archived, recalled, or replayed. They are usually added to accommodate requirements for integrity verification or prediction of future behavior.

- *Agents*—Represent active proxies for actors. An actor may set up an agent that acts in its stead. The agent must be capable of receiving the system's outputs and responding appropriately according to the policy and instructions determined by the actor.

There are two general techniques for identifying the additional classes and relationships needed for application analysis. They are described below and are often performed together.

DOMAIN ANALYSIS REFINEMENT

THE TECHNIQUE OF domain analysis refinement involves examining the outputs from domain analysis (object, dynamic, functional models) and the outputs from conceptualization (problem statement, context diagram, operations concepts, high-level use cases) and identifying all opportunities for application classes. This approach usually starts with each application class opportunity and then designs the class in visible user terms (e.g., display, application, menu), based on the operations concepts determined in conceptualization. By placing these on the domain model, and by defining and specifying their behavior, we produce an application model.

USE-CASE REFINEMENT

ANOTHER POPULAR WAY to begin application analysis is to take each use case in turn and define the details of the interchange between the actor and the system. At each interchange of events, we consider opportunities for application classes. As each use case is finished, we can construct a separate application model for each use case, or combine them all into one application model.

SURROGATES

IT IS USEFUL to distinguish at this time between the physical, real-world objects and the software objects that represent them. Examine the domain model from the previous chapter, focusing on the actor Student. The Student is certainly within our system, but the actual student is not within the software application. The two aspects of the Student class need to be separated; one is the internal software data object that keeps track of our information on the student as a surrogate, and the other is the active actor class.[1]

Generally, the actor objects include operations for sending and receiving data to and from the system. For human actors, these correspond to the steps and procedures that the user must perform (e.g., enter data). The actors also have attributes that correspond to state information. For users, the attributes are the things they should know (e.g., their name). The surrogate objects usually have the same attributes, but typically, they only have access operations. The surrogate often a has a few extra attributes to indicate the state of the actor from the system's point of view, or to help identify particular surrogates.

There are several techniques for distinguishing both types of objects within the system. The simplest is to change the name of the surrogate object in some standard way, such as to append the word Info, e.g., StudentInfo. We can expect to have equivalent surrogate objects for the other actors, Administrator and Professor. There

---

[1] Both Student classes need to be traced. The actor Student needs to be modeled to understand the actions and activities the student is asked to perform and the constraints the student must obey to use this system. The Student information includes very little behavior, but we must understand what attributes that the system needs to keep track of the actor.

might also be surrogate objects for the more passive real-world objects, such as Course.

Another technique for distinguishing surrogates from the physical objects is to flag the surrogate object by placing a class property field in the attribute section. A class property indicator looks like an attribute, but is preceded by the '!' symbol.

ADDING SURROGATES IN RATIONAL ROSE

1. Create a new class diagram by choosing Class Diagram . . . from the Browse menu.
2. Double-click on < New >, enter the name of the diagram, and click the OK button.
3. Add the actor classes to this diagram by choosing Add Classes . . . from the Query menu. From the resulting dialog, select the actors that are to be added to this diagram. Select the OK button.
4. Create the new surrogate classes as you would any new class, starting by selecting the class icon from the tool palette.
5. Name the new classes to distinguish them from the actors (e.g., StudentInfo).
6. Place the previously identified attributes on the new surrogate class. If desired, add the class property indicator !surrogate to the surrogate class as an attribute and an equivalent !actor to the actor class.
7. Using the association icon from the tool palette, draw an association connecting the actor class with its surrogate.

Since the software development team is primarily interested in the surrogate objects and not the actors, gradually move the actors out of the application model and into their own category. This keeps them out of the way, but still available when needed. When the user's procedures and manuals are designed, they will be of prime importance.

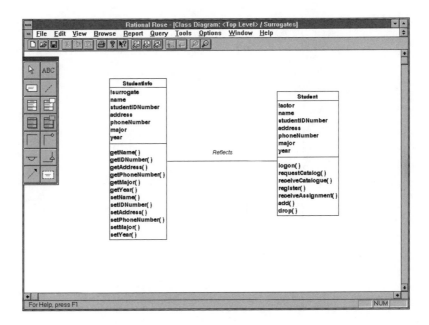

CREATING CATEGORIES IN RATIONAL ROSE

1. Display the previously created < Top Level > /Main class diagram by choosing Class Diagram . . . from the Browse menu and selecting the diagram from the list of diagrams.
2. On this diagram, create a new category by selecting the category icon (dashed rectangle) and placing it on the diagram.
3. While the category is selected, type the name of the category.

MOVING CLASSES IN RATIONAL ROSE

1. Double-click on the category icon to create a Main class diagram within the category.
2. Add the actor classes to this diagram by choosing Add Classes . . . from the Query menu.
3. From the resulting dialog, select the Category where the classes to be moved currently reside.

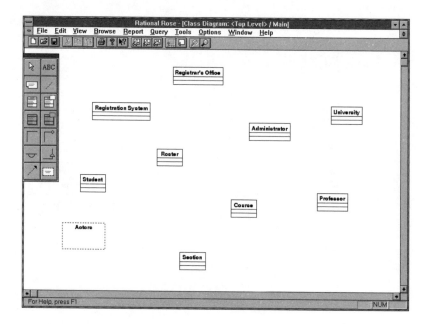

4. Select the actors and bring them over to the Selected Classes list by selecting the > > > > button.
5. Click the OK button.
6. While the classes are still selected, select the Relocate menu option from the Edit menu.

SYSTEM AND APPLICATION CONTROLLERS

WHEN LOOKING AT the problem from the use-case point of view, it is useful to identify objects that represent the system as a whole as well as individual applications within the system. These objects are technically controller objects, because they control the sequence and conduct of the system. There are other types of controllers, so these application-controller objects are usually called *applications,* for generally that is what they are.

For convenience, a first cut is to just consider a system object. This object, RegistrationSystem, was already identified during the conceptualization phase. If further refinement is needed, we might hypothesize separate application objects for each actor. It seems

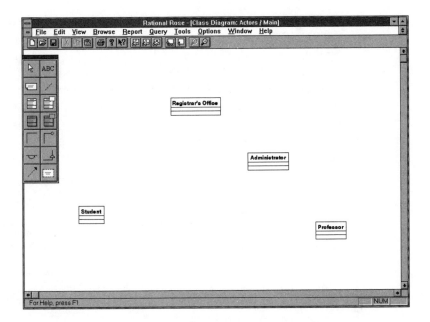

likely that the Student would bring up a different application than the Professor, and that both would bring up a different application than the Administrator. Each application would present the user with significantly different choices and options, so that it would be best at this phase to consider them independent. It may also be useful to create lower-level application objects for each use case. A category for the application-controller classes is created and added to the application model.

VIEWS AND PRESENTATIONS

WHEN AN ACTOR is presented with information, that information itself is not the actual object within the system. It is a view, perhaps not complete, of a domain object, domain association, controller, or a combination of them. It has a form of its own and is an object in its own right. Identify the views during application analysis as their construction is a significant aspect of system development. Each report, output screen, or representation should be identified for requirements, costing, and scheduling purposes.

The course registration problem includes several easily identified families of views. Though the need for a view can be identified by the appearance of any output to any actor, it is a requirements issue to determine the form, frequency, and usability of the view. A practical way of determining these requirements is to prototype the view layouts and allow user focus groups to review them. The views should be named with terms that users would typically use, as in the accompanying table.

Sample Views to the Student

Underlying Object	View Name	Potential Descriptions
Course-Information	Catalog	Printed and mailed form, includes several different views (e.g., full description in course number order; additional lists in day/time order; perhaps precedence graphs of prerequisites)
	Course Screens	List of courses, sortable by several fields (title, dept, number, location, professor)
Course-Student relationship (Assignment)	Assignment Screen	List form, sortable by course number or date/time, blocked-out weekly schedule form. Campus map with highlighted rooms
	Course Assignment	Similar to screen forms, but tailored to paper; perhaps a printed mailed form for legal purposes

INTERFACES

INTERFACE CLASSES HANDLE information that crosses system boundaries; they convert or reformat information for interpretation by the destination system. When a printer is used, the classes that convert a view to Postscript for sending to the Printer device would be interface classes. Interfaces are also associated with input to the system. Input forms or menus, whether paper or screens, are often considered as interfaces to the system.

SUMMARY

APPLICATION MODELS ARE built on top of the domain models to capture the required system as seen by the users. One of the ways of doing this is to examine the domain model and the outputs from conceptualization and to look for opportunities to create application classes. Such application classes are not part of the essential domain, but they are visible to the users. They include views, presentations, interface classes, controllers, devices, reifications, and agents. After identifying the need for these classes, we design the classes by determining the form in which they will appear to the users: reports, screens, menus, and so forth.

Look at each actor and other domain objects to determine if the system needs a surrogate to track it. Create controllers for the applications or use cases that the actor participates in. Then, for each communication from the actor, identify the need for an interface object(s) to translate or transform the communication into the system. For communications to the actor, consider views and presentations. Create views for those domain objects, associations, or application controllers that the actor may want to see. Look at each event or request to determine if it needs to be reviewed or undone.

GLOSSARY

ACCESS OPERATION

An operation that gets or sets an object's attributes or associations.

AGENT

An active proxy for an actor. It responds to the system's outputs and supplies the actor's normal inputs.

APPLICATION MODELING

The application model describes the behavior of the system as seen by the users. It includes the visible part of the design solution, including such computer constructs as screens, menus, and reports.

APPLICATION OBJECTS

The visible solution classes required for the system.

CONTROLLER CLASSES

Controllers control applications and user interfaces, and also manage relationships.

DEVICE CLASSES

The physical devices and the software surrogate classes that encapsulate communication to the physical devices.

INTERFACE CLASSES

Classes that transform, translate, or format inputs that cross system or media boundaries.

REIFICATION CLASSES

Classes that represent events, functions, communications, or operations that are being treated as objects for the purpose of reviewing, previewing, undoing, or redoing.

SURROGATE CLASSES

Classes that represent the internal system view of a domain class.

VIEW CLASSES

Classes that present an appearance of some subject to an actor.

Chapter 23

Application Use-Case Analysis

- Use Cases

- Scenarios

- Message Trace Diagrams

- Scenario Analysis

- Summary

- Glossary

USE CASES

MORE INFORMATION IS added to the object model during detailed analysis of use cases. A use case is a pattern of use of the system by an actor—a family of scenarios bound together by common use. The collection of use cases describes the system functions of the application. The high-level use cases have already been identified in the conceptualization phase. Now we examine each use case in more detail and extract the detail to develop the application model and application requirements.

SCENARIOS

THE RECOMMENDED WAY of exploring the detail of a use case is to start with a scenario, that is, a specific sequence of events being exchanged. First start with the primary, or most likely, scenario. Then add secondary scenarios. Finally, add error, or exception scenarios. Do not identify all possible scenarios but attempt to capture the equivalence cases, that is, the scenarios that illustrate the qualitative differences in behavior.

MESSAGE TRACE DIAGRAMS

IT IS OFTEN useful to graphically depict a scenario, using a message trace diagram to capture the pattern of interactions for each one. In the message trace diagram, columns are used to indicate the participating objects in the scenario, usually with the actor(s) to the left.

A message trace diagram shows the events and messages passing among the objects by the use of ordered, labeled arrows. During analysis, we concentrate on the events, the logical notifications of happenings, as opposed to operations, which involve implied transfer of control. Events may communicate data, or they may be pure signals. Design develops the mappings between these logical events and the detailed operations.

CREATING MESSAGE TRACE
DIAGRAMS IN RATIONAL ROSE

1. Choose Scenario Diagram from the Browse menu option.
2. Double-click on < New > to display the New Scenario window.
3. Type the name of the scenario in the Name field of the New Scenario window.
4. Confirm that Message Trace is the selected option.
5. Click the OK button.

The New Scenario window follows.

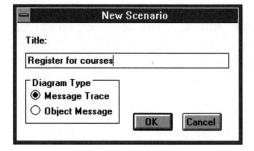

CREATING OBJECTS AND MESSAGES IN
MESSAGE TRACE DIAGRAMS IN RATIONAL ROSE

1. Click to select the object icon (rectangle) from the tool palette.
2. Click on the diagram window.
3. Type the name of the object in the rectangle.
4. Double-click on the object to make the Object Specification window visible.

5. Attach the object to a class by selecting the class name from the Class pulldown menu.
6. Repeat the above steps for each object in the scenario.
7. Click to select the message icon (arrow) from the tool palette.
8. Move the mouse pointer to the line for the sending object, click on the object sending the message in the diagram window, and drag the line to the receiving object.
9. To create the message and make the message an operation of the receiving class, click the right mouse button on the receiving class.
10. Select either an existing operation or a new operation.
11. If new operation is selected, type the name of the operation in the Name field of the Operation Specification.
12. To make the newly created operation visible, click the right mouse button and select the operation from the list of operations.

The following message trace diagram shown on page 248 shows the scenario of registering for a course where the four primary choices are valid.

An optional script detailing the scenario in words may be added to a message trace diagram in order to provide additional documentation. A script may be written in free-form text, structured text, or the chosen implementation language.

CREATING SCRIPTS IN RATIONAL ROSE
1. Select the text icon (ABC) from the tool palette.
2. Click on the diagram and type the text for the script.
3. Resize the text if necessary.
4. Click on the text, depress the shift key, and click on the message for the script.
5. Choose the Attach Script menu option from the Edit menu.

The modified message trace diagram follows.

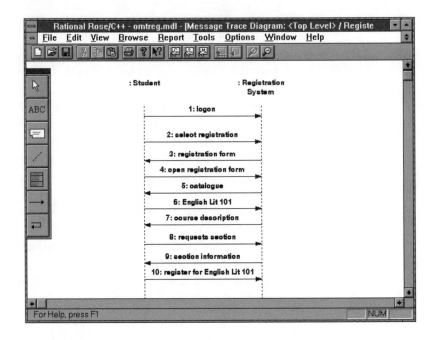

SCENARIO ANALYSIS

TO PERFORM APPLICATION analysis based on this scenario, start with the scenario description and message trace and treat them as if they were a problem statement for domain analysis. The same essential techniques used previously are now applied to this new problem with the benefit of a better understanding from all the previous work (e.g., conceptualization and the previous domain model).

Though it can be a separate step, most of the time this domain analysis of the scenario is combined with some amount of application analysis. For example, whenever the model indicates that an actor is shown the state of some object, it is possible to deduce that there are two objects, the domain object and the *view* of the domain object.

SUMMARY

BUILD APPLICATION MODELS on top of the domain models to capture the required system as seen by the users. We do this by examining

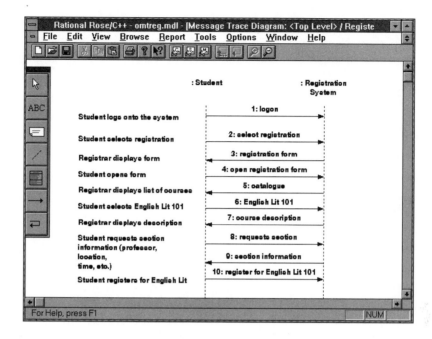

the use cases developed earlier. Each use case is expanded to contain a set or web of scenarios. As the scenarios are developed, the classes and behavior needed to perform the function of the scenario are added to the object model or are already externally visible. After identifying the need for these classes, "design" them by determining the form that they will appear to the users, as reports, screens, menus, etc.

GLOSSARY

MESSAGE TRACE DIAGRAM

A columnar diagram that graphically shows the interactions among objects in a scenario.

SCENARIO

A particular path through the system, expressed in terms of interactions among objects.

Chapter 24

Generalization

GENERALIZATION

AS ANALYSIS PROGRESSES, it becomes necessary to organize and simplify the model. Though it can be performed at any time, this process is usually delayed until enough details are found to detect commonalities. In object-oriented systems, besides *association* and *aggregation,* there is a special relationship that may exist among classes. This relationship, called *generalization,* is used as an organized sharing (or reusing) of features among the classes. A class that defines the common structure *(attributes),* behavior *(operations),* relationships *(associations),* and meaning for a set of classes is the *generalization* of the set of classes. This generalization class, often called the *superclass,* defines a basis for the remaining classes *(subclasses)* and is an abstraction of them. Each subclass *inherits* the properties of its superclass but may also extend the inherited properties with its own properties. Because any class may be a subclass, it is possible to have a whole hierarchy of classes. Subclasses inherit the properties defined in any of the superclasses defined higher in the generalization.[1]

This process of finding the common abstraction and making a superclass, of moving from the specific to the abstract, is similar to the process by which humans make sense of common objects. Just as we examine objects in the real world to find classes by abstraction and classification, analysts examine classes to find superclasses by abstraction and generalization.

The process that goes the other way, that of starting with a class and making specialized versions *(subclasses),* called *specialization,* is also performed. Specialization usually adds or modifies existing behavior based on the specialized purposes of the subclass, adds new attributes to track new information or states of the specialized subclass, or adds new associations to map new relationships of the

---

[1] During analysis, classes usually inherit from only one direct superclass (single inheritance), which may in turn inherit from only one direct superclass, but it is possible to inherit from more that one class. If a class shares the structure defined in more than one inheritance hierarchy, it has what is called *multiple inheritance.*

subclass.[2] Though both specialization and generalization are used during object-oriented development, generalization is the more common process, especially during analysis.

THE GENERALIZATION PROCESS

WE LOOK OVER the analysis models with an eye for generalization throughout the analysis process, as well as later throughout the design phase. Whenever we find two or more classes that seem similar in structure, behavior, relationships, and purposes, we examine in detail the potential for extracting commonality. It is important to look for synonyms or near synonyms. Two classes may have identical properties under different names, or two classes may have identically named properties that are actually different.

Inheritance is often misused. One way of checking whether inheritance is appropriate is by verifying that the subclass "is-a" member of the superclass. If an instance of the subclass cannot substitute for the superclass, that is, if it is not a "kind-of" the superclass, then inheritance is not being properly used.

GENERALIZATION IN THE COURSE REGISTRATION PROBLEM

THE COURSE REGISTRATION problem offers several opportunities for generalization. For example, there are common attributes and operations belonging to Professor and Student. A new superclass, RegUser (Registration User), is created to hold the common structure (attributes), behavior (operations), and relationships (associations), while the unique features remain in the proper places in the Student and Professor classes. To properly generalize, common features must be determined, and potential differences need to be reconciled. We need to ask such as questions as the following: "Are the attributes studentID and employeeID the same? Can the attributes be treated

---

[2] In some circumstances, the analyst may hide or significantly modify the behavior or structure of the superclass when specializing. However, this violates the "is-a" nature of good object-oriented inheritance.

the same, or are they essentially different?[3] Besides evaluating the attributes, we examine the operations that the Student and the Professor have to perform in their respective use cases. Does the Student request a Catalog, or receive a Catalog, in the same way that the Professor does? The more the operations and attributes are similar, the more useful generalization will be, and the simpler it will be to develop the application (and the user manual). It may be necessary to modify the names or interpretations of some attributes or operations to a common form for better generalization. The Student and Professor classes are added as subclasses to the RegUser generalization hierarchy.

CREATING GENERALIZATIONS IN RATIONAL ROSE

1. Create a new class (the superclass) by using the class icon from the tool palette. Place it above the subclass(es) on the class diagram.
2. Select the generalization icon (the line with a surcharged triangle) from the tool palette.
3. Click on one of the subclasses and drag the generalization line to the superclass.
4. Select the generalization icon again from the tool palette, click another subclass, and drag the line to the previously created generalization symbol (the triangle).
5. Repeat step 4 for each additional subclass.
6. Double click on the superclass and add all the common attributes and operations.
7. Double click on each subclass and delete any attributes and operations that have been placed on the superclass.

---

[3] Treating the student and the employee IDs as the same may cause problems in real life. In the United States, Social Security numbers are often used for both, but students are allowed to choose otherwise for better privacy. If the attributes are combined, then students who are also professors lose this privilege. This reminds us that attributes of real objects may have use outside of the system. Generally, separate internal IDs from external names.

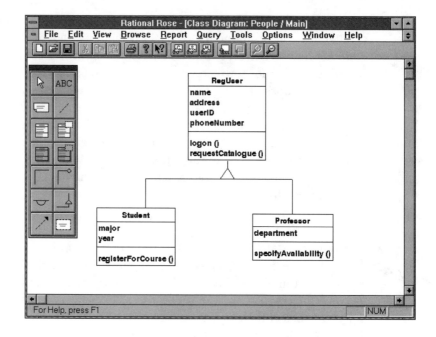

SUMMARY

AFTER HAVING IDENTIFIED classes, we can look for generalization opportunities to capture the common features from classes. For classes with common structure (attributes), behavior (operations), relationships (associations) and meaning, we can make a new class, a superclass, to hold these common features and leave only the unique features in the previously existing classes, now called *subclasses*.

GLOSSARY

GENERALIZATION

> The process (and resulting structure) that abstracts commonality in structure, behavior, and relationships from a set of classes.

INHERITANCE

The sharing of features from a superclass with its subclasses in a generalization hierarchy.

"IS-A" RELATIONSHIP

Another name for the generalization relationship that emphasizes that a subclass must be a kind of a superclass, and the subclass must be able to be substituted for the superclass.

SPECIALIZATION

The process that takes a class and, by refinement, creates variant subclasses.

SUBCLASS

A subclass "is-a" variant of the superclass. It inherits from its superclass in a generalization hierarchy.

SUPERCLASS

A parent class in a generalization hierarchy that defines the common features of the subclasses and acts as the basis for the subclass variants.

Chapter 25

Analysis:
Functional Modeling

FUNCTIONAL MODELING

FUNCTIONAL MODELING IS the third leg of the triad of views of the system. The OMT functional model attempts to enumerate, capture, and describe the operations and their effects on the objects within (and perhaps outside) the system. The functional model is also used to specify algorithmic and performance requirements. There are two aspects or viewpoints to functional modeling.

During domain analysis, we identify the system-level operations and fundamental operations on the domain objects. Other than identifying them and describing them in the model dictionary, the context diagram and use-case diagram are usually sufficient for functional modeling needs.

In the course registration problem, there is not much need for a diagrammed, analysis-level functional model, because much of the information has already been captured in other, already produced artifacts. For example, the context diagram serves to capture some of the high-level dataflow between the actors and the system. The high-level use cases identified are the high-level system functions. The fundamental communications associated with the use cases are the dataflows associated with these system functions.

OPERATION SPECIFICATIONS

IT IS SOMETIMES necessary to explore the steps of a use case to capture more detailed requirements. If so, we construct scenarios to establish the steps that are performed in the use case. Then, by treating the steps as operations, we can specify algorithmic and performance requirements at the appropriate level.

ADDING FUNCTIONAL INFORMATION
TO AN OPERATION SPECIFICATION

1. Display the Class Specification window by double-clicking on the class.

2. Double-click on the operation name to make the Operation Specification window visible.
3. Type the functional requirements for the operation in the Documentation field.
4. Enter any needed pre- or postconditions.

The operation specification for the verifyPassword operation follows.

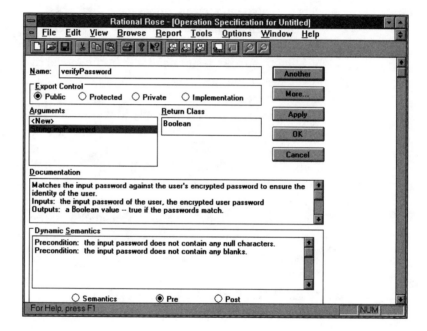

SUMMARY

THOUGH THE OBJECT and dynamic models are generally more important, the functional model is still necessary for complete understanding of the system to be constructed. We use the functional model to capture algorithmic and performance requirements by constructing operation specifications.

GLOSSARY

FUNCTIONAL CONSTRAINT

> Either a precondition or postcondition that a transformation must obey.

OPERATION SPECIFICATION

> A textual description of an operation following the project template that captures the purpose, transformation, and functional constraints of an operation. During design, it may capture the procedural flow of the operation.

POSTCONDITION

> A constraint on the outputs that must hold if the preconditions were met.

PRECONDITION

> A constraint on inputs and starting circumstances that must hold at initiation if the use case or function is to finish successfully. If a precondition does not hold, the results are unpredictable.

Chapter 26

Testing

THE NEED FOR TESTING

NO PART OF the development process can successfully be completed without being tested. If system development is a journey to the best system that can be found with given resources and time, testing is the checking of the compass and map to ensure that the way hasn't been lost. Testing is also the scouting ahead to check that our goal is still desirable and feasible along this path.

Testing includes the continuous and periodic checking of the following:

- **Consistency**—Are the products developed in this phase consistent (noncontradictory) with each other?

- **Requirements satisfaction**—Do the developed products address all input requirements?

- **Client satisfaction**—Is the client satisfied with the project's direction and progress?

- **Sufficiency**—Are the developed products sufficient for development to continue in the next phase?

- **Necessity**—Do the developed products minimize duplicate specifications while covering all perspectives? Do the developed products postpone decisions to their appropriate phase with no overspecification?

- **Flexibility**—Are the developed products capable of addressing reasonable design and contingency variations?

- **Format**—Do the developed products meet the project's format and style requirements?

- **Traceability**—Have the decisions that were made to get to this point been sufficiently documented?

Because OMT development involves multiple views of a system, each view requires checks to ensure consistency with the others. Each view is an opportunity to gather alternative insight into the system, whether this is done by several teams simultaneously or by one team in series. Testing is even more important when many people are involved, as there is more opportunity for inconsistency. Progress on each view usually requires changes to the other views.

MODEL WALKTHROUGHS

EACH MODEL REQUIRES a team examination to verify that the model makes sense and is consistent. As each model diagram is finished and work progresses to new material, we need to hold a team-based review of the developed products, including a review of the diagram(s), its associated model dictionary, and the major inputs to the process that produced the diagram(s).

It is often useful to develop a model narrative for each model diagram that describes the diagram's meaning. A narrative is simply the description that would be given when presenting the diagram in detail. The narrative should not say anything that is not on the diagram; if the statements in the narrative are numbered, they form a basis that facilitates requirements testing and tracking. As the narrative is developed, it is reviewed along with its diagrams.

The review should check for consistency among the model, the narrative, and the form of the products. It should also check that the input requirements are met, and that design decisions have been captured and justified.

MODEL DICTIONARY CHECKING

EVERY MODEL FEATURE must be defined in the model dictionary. All terms used in the inputs to this phase (for example, nouns and verbs) must be in the model dictionary, equivalent to something in the dictionary or some "noise" term acting as filler. The definition must be clear and concise, and two different terms should not have the same names.[1] Any terms used in the model dictionary must also be defined.

---

[1] It is not always possible to avoid having terms that share names. In this case, the terms should be employed in different scopes (e.g., categories).

USE-CASE SCENARIO WALKTHROUGHS

ONE TECHNIQUE THAT appears very valuable is to walk through use-case scenarios by role-playing the objects and actors. As each event is sent, the person playing the receiving object (or actor) determines which of its operations needs to be initiated, or whether the responsibility to handle this event is better delegated to some other object. Operations and events so identified are placed on the object models, and the scenario diagram and state charts are updated.

This technique is generally most suited for designing the responsibilities of the objects, but it does offer some analysis value, because it can identify the need for new objects, actors, and events. When performed with the real user representatives playing the actors, along with prototype software, it can verify that the use cases are feasible and acceptable.

MODEL CONSISTENCY

BECAUSE THE MODELS offer different views of the domain and different views of the application, the views may not be completely consistent. Entities appearing in one model may appear in a different model by a different name, or may not appear at all. Entities might need to be mapped to a different form before they can appear in another model. By the time analysis is finished, these consistency problems may be significant. Though resolving these consistency problems may often be left to the end of analysis, it is better if this part of testing is continuously applied.

Often a feature in one model needs to be mapped to a different form before it appears in another model. For example, sending an event usually corresponds to the calling of an operation on the receiving object. Checking this correspondence is useful in analysis, but we should be aware that the exact mapping is part of the design. It may be possible to send an event from one object to another by several other techniques, such as the return of an operation, an interrupt, polling, and so on. Choosing the technique is properly part of design.

PATH AND QUERY TESTING

ONE TECHNIQUE THAT is often applied to checking class diagrams is to construct typical queries and check that the model can answer those queries by offering a path to the necessary information. For example, in order for a student to take a course with a prerequisite, the student must have a passing grade for all prerequisite courses. At this point in time, the Registration System does not model any grade information. A grade class is created and added to the model as shown in the following class diagram.

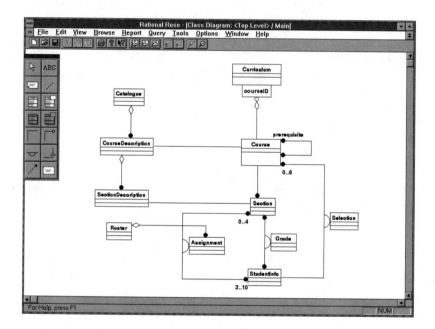

REQUIREMENTS TRACEABILITY

IF FORMAL REQUIREMENTS are available for this project, testing includes tracing each requirement to the class(es), association, constraint, and operation(s) that satisfy the requirement. For smaller projects, the requirement or requirement ID may be added to the model dictionary entry for each class. For larger or more formal projects, a commercial requirements tool or database management system (DBMS) may be used. For projects without formal requirements, it is should be possible to walk through each output item from conceptualization and check whether it is captured in the analysis output.

USER AND CLIENT INVOLVEMENT

CLIENT AND USER representatives should participate in all stages of verification. Though we run the risk of getting new requirements from this involvement, it is better to get them now than to have the project rejected at delivery. It is not necessary for these people to participate in every review and walkthrough, but the external reviewers should be chosen to match the product being reviewed. For example, domain experts should be involved throughout the domain analysis, and users' representatives should be involved during use-case analysis.

SUMMARY

TESTING IS REQUIRED for all developed products. Different types of testing are performed as appropriate for the product being evaluated. Involving the users in testing and approval improves the quality and acceptance of the product.

GLOSSARY

MODEL CONSISTENCY CHECKING
>   The process of ensuring that the information found in the three OMT models, (object, dynamic, and functional) are telling the same story.

REQUIREMENTS TRACEABILITY
>   The ability to determine for each requirement the analysis, design, and implementation elements that contribute to meeting that requirement and that would be affected if the requirement changed.

Chapter 27

System Design

THE NEED FOR SYSTEM DESIGN

AFTER DETERMINING THE system's requirements, we need to determine the overall approach to the solution, its system architecture, and style. This activity is called system design, and it includes the following tasks.

- Partitioning the system into subsystems

- Allocating subsystems to components (e.g., hardware, software, and operations)

- Assigning subsystems to teams

- Determining the architectural framework for each subsystem

- Identifying concurrency, tasks, and the approach to control for each subsystem

- Establishing policy for error handling, boundary conditions, system safety, integrity, and security issues

- Choosing approaches for handling global resources, persistent data, human-machine interfaces, and so on.

- Prioritizing system goals and requirements to support local design decisions and trade-offs

- Organizing system capabilities into releases

- Scheduling releases

PARTITIONING INTO SUBSYSTEMS

MOST SYSTEMS ARE large enough to require partitioning into smaller logical components, or subsystems. Such a *divide and conquer strategy* makes it easier to address each subsystem, not only because of its smaller size, but also because the component can be made more uniform and comprehensible. A subsystem is a logical collection of classes that are themselves highly cohesive, but loosely coupled to other classes. The partitioning of subsystems should be based on their sharing some common property, for example, similar functionality, common physical location, or common implementation approaches. By packaging a group of interrelated classes, associations, operations, events, and constraints into a subsystem, we aim to produce a tightly coupled independent entity.

Subsystems are typically chosen in a way that organizes our systems into distinct layers and partitions. A layer denotes classes at the same level of abstraction—a horizontal slice that provides the basis for the layers above it. A partition denotes a vertical slice— weakly coupled or independent applications. Typical systems use both principles of division: layers to encapsulate the system from dependencies on hardware or other lower-level implementation choices, and partitions to allow independent development of applications based on common subsystems. Large subsystems may themselves be decomposed by the same principles. Subsystems may also be constructed to contain delivery-specific or use-case-specific components. The client organization should also be able to build the subsystems—it does no good to blindly follow a logical breakdown if the organization's team structure (e.g., size, composition, culture) cannot be modified to work with it.

In the ESU course registration problem, there are several choices for subsystems. For example, the surrogate classes and other domain classes (excluding the actors themselves) are tightly coupled, generally persistent, and form one subsystem. The registration system itself is another subsystem, perhaps with each application controller forming a sub-subsystem. The user interface forms another subsystem. Some developers would also group the actors together and consider them another subsystem.

Subsystems may have relationships to each other. A subsystem is said "to use," or to be a client of, another subsystem when it relies on services exported by the other, *server* subsystem or has knowledge of the server subsystem. This "uses" relationship may be drawn with a dashed arrow from the client subsystem to server subsystem. The relationship may be named to further clarify its purpose. Two subsystems may use each other in a *peer-to-peer* relationship. Some utility subsystems may be used by almost every other subsystem, so that they would be considered *global*. An important part of system design is to plan the relationships and communications between subsystems.

If large enough, each subsystem may be considered a system of its own and divided into additional subsystems. These subsystems are contained within the parent subsystem and are usually not visible from outside of the containing parent.

CREATING SUBSYSTEMS
(CATEGORIES) IN RATIONAL ROSE

1. Select the category icon (rectangle) from the palette.
2. Click on the diagram to draw the category (dashed rectangle).
3. Type the name of the category inside the category icon.
4. Repeat steps 2 through 4 for each category.
5. Select the "uses" relationship icon (the dashed arrow) from the palette.
6. Draw the arrow from the client (using) to the server (used) category.

The category diagram for the registration system follows on page 278.

ALLOCATING SUBSYSTEMS

TO IMPLEMENT A subsystem, we must allocate it to a physical implementation approach. Each subsystem's approach needs to be determined before detailed design may proceed. At the high level, the implementation approaches can be software, hardware, or operations (the people side). Software approaches can be further specified as follows:

- *Developed in-house:* Language should also be specified

- *Commercial-off-the-shelf (COTS) Package:* Class libraries, routines, or executables

- *Framework:* In-house or commercially available framework

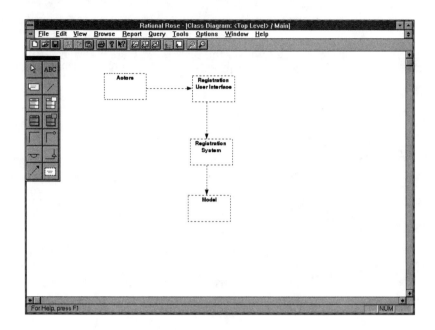

- *Legacy package:* In-house, on-hand software

- *Public domain package:* Publicly available software with risk

- *Specially developed/qualified software:* For example, trusted, reusable, portable, and exportable

- *Logical Location:* Client, server, as an applet or plug-in

If not predetermined, the number, grade, and capabilities of the hardware must be specified:

- *Printers, Plotters:* Pages per minute, color, fonts

- *Terminals, monitors:* Color, size, refresh ratio

- *Local clients:* O/S version, windowing environment, speed, memory, disk space

- *Servers:* O/S version, speed, memory, disk space

- *Communication devices:* Modem protocols, speed, encryption, compression

- *Network and network hardware:* Ethernet, token ring, speed, copper, fiber

For operations, we need to know the number, capabilities, and requirements of each role (or job position). We must be sure that these specifications are justified by the requirements. Overly restrictive job requirements will make it difficult to hire people and leave the organization potentially open to discrimination suits. We examine the operations that have been assigned to each actor to determine the requirements. Any restrictions created should be carefully understood, and the driving operation descriptions and design should be reevaluated to be as open as possible.

- *Education:* High school, some college

- *Experience:* Number of years

- *Specific training/ratings:* Typing wpm, can lift x pounds

- *Required abilities:* Can use phone, can use computer, can distinguish colors

Capturing Allocation

There are several ways of capturing these allocations; for example, see the Rose-supplied Booch capabilities to document processors, devices, subsystems, and modules, as described in the Booch part of this book. Another popular approach is to use class diagrams to show the subsystems, processors, and connections among them. With this approach, we use associations to capture the "uses" or "runs on" relationships, aggregations to capture "composed of" or "contains" relationships, operations to capture capabilities and running software, and attributes to capture specifications and static requirements. Class and role multiplicities are also used in this approach to establish the sizing parameters for the subsystem architecture. The following architecture diagram is an example.

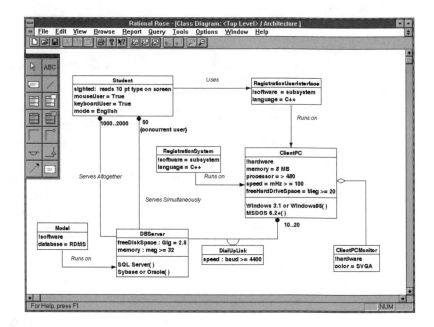

POLICY DECISIONS

DURING SYSTEM DESIGN, policy decisions to guide detailed design are made. Some of the decisions needed for this system are discussed below.

Error-Handling and Boundary Conditions Policy

A standard error-handling policy and level of usability must be decided upon. Because the users are not expected to be experts (they only use the software once a semester), the system needs to target naive users. If there are only twenty fixed locations for client terminals and about fifteen hundred users, extra care should be taken to be sure that no error can hang up a terminal, as each terminal represents a significant part of the system's resources. With a large number of users expected per day, rebooting a client PC must be easy, quick, and not disturbing to the rest of the users.

Risk Mitigation: Safety, Integrity, and Security Policy
There is significant risk to a university if this system does not work;
therefore, a back-up registration contingency plan should exist. It
may be necessary to keep the paper-based system available as a
potential backup. This would be useful in case of significant software
failures, as well as hardware or power problems.

By having a login and password scheme, the integrity of the system has been partially addressed. A security policy should also be
determined. For example, should students be able to see other students' registration records?

ADDITIONAL SYSTEM DESIGN DECISIONS

AS PART OF the general policy decisions, the mechanisms to enforce
these decisions must also be determined. These usually involve specifying subsystems that implement the policy, which may be built,
borrowed (reused), or bought, and are usually globally available as
subsystems or class libraries. In the university, for example, the following implementation subsystems are needed:

- GUI widgets

- DB interface

- Error handling

- Foundation classes

- Database

- Hardware

The architecture team needs to specify how these will be provided: whether by newly written subsystems, commercial class
libraries, or some other mechanism. Then the subsystem category
diagram would be updated to reflect any new subsystems, and the
subsystem allocation (class) diagram would be updated to show any
new running applications.

MAKING A CATEGORY GLOBAL IN RATIONAL ROSE
1. Click on the category in the class diagram.
2. Choose Specification from the Browse menu to open the Category Specification window.
3. Check the global box.
4. Click the OK button.

The updated subsystem category class diagram follows.

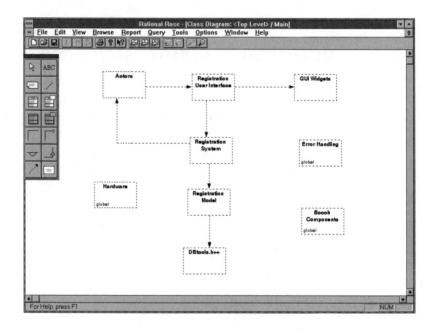

Populating the Subsystems

Once the categories/subsystems have been created, the original classes must be moved to the appropriate categories. We must examine each class to determine the best category for it. When the population of the subsystems with the classes is finished, there should be no classes left in the Top Level category.

Determining System/Subsystem Interfaces

To encourage independent development of systems and subsystems, we need to establish the interfaces among them early. For each subsystem-to-subsystem interface, we determine the classes that offer public services that are used by other subsystems.

SHOWING PUBLIC CLASSES IN RATIONAL ROSE

1. Click the right mouse button on the category in the class diagram.
2. Select Edit Compartment.
3. Select the public classes.
4. Click < < > > to move the classes to the Selected Classes dialogue box.
5. Click the OK button.

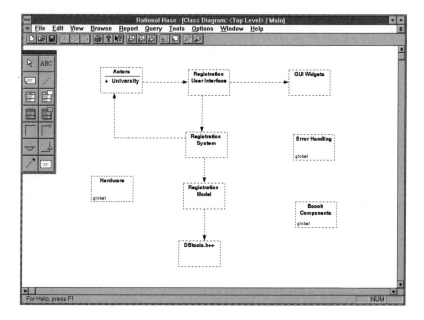

RELEASE PLANNING

AS SYSTEM DESIGN nears completion, it is necessary to revisit scheduling. It is usually not desirable to attempt to produce the whole system with all its capabilities at one time. Instead, we choose some portion of the system to do first, schedule the remaining phases for that portion, and perhaps even ship it to the field. Other portions of the system can be developed in parallel, slightly delayed, or even postponed until results from the first system are seen.

As the design for a subsystem becomes known, it becomes feasible to determine the implementation time, required resources, and inter-subsystem dependencies. The first few releases are usually layers, because they serve as bases for remaining subsystems and need to be developed first. In the ESU course registration problem, the database subsystem and the applications needed to populate the database (add courses, students, professors) would probably be done first. Later releases are often partitions, usually in the form of use cases. Adding a new use case adds a complete, testable capability. The student registration use cases would probably be developed before the add and drop use cases. In some circumstances, a new operations concept for a use case will be added. For example, we might field the registration system on dedicated PC clients before we allow dial-up.

SUMMARY

SYSTEM DESIGN BUILDS on the operations concepts determined in conceptualization and the application classes determined in analysis to produce the system architecture, where the major components (software, hardware, and operations) are specified. Subsystems are identified, populated with classes, and allocated to processors. Policy decisions on how to handle common issues, such as error handling, and GUI look and feel are made, and system components are designed to implement them. The order and schedule for the development and release of the subsystems are planned.

GLOSSARY

ARCHITECTURE DIAGRAM

A class diagram that shows the major components of a system: the hardware, logical subsystems, operations personnel, and the relationships among them. The diagram is also used to specify implementation requirements, component multiplicity, running applications, and other major architecture decisions.

CLIENT-SERVER

A relationship between system components where one component offers services (often request/response) to other components. The clients need to know how to contact the server and how to request the service; thus, they depend on or use the server.

GLOBAL SUBSYSTEM

A subsystem that is visible to all other subsystems and classes enclosed within the same subsystem.

INTEGRITY POLICY

The approach taken to limiting changes to a system to authorized changes with a proper audit trail.

LAYER

The collection of class categories or subsystems at the same level of abstraction.

OPERATIONS

The part of the system that is performed by humans. Humans may have responsibilities as actors, interface objects, controllers, or even processors, depending on the system.

PARTITION

The class categories or subsystems that form a part of a given level of abstraction.

PEER-TO-PEER

> The cooperative relationship between system components (e.g., subsystems) where both subsystems depend on each other.

SAFETY POLICY

> The approach taken to preventing system-caused damage to life, property, or reputation. The policy needs to consider internal failure (e.g., software bugs, design flaws) and externally caused failures (e.g., user error, power outages).

SECURITY POLICY

> The approach taken to guarding information, so that it is available only for properly authorized viewing.

SUBSYSTEM DIAGRAM

> A class diagram that shows the major subsystems of a system and their relationships.

SYSTEM DESIGN

> The activity during system development that formalizes the system architecture, system policies, and release planning.

Chapter 28

Object Design

OBJECT DESIGN

AS OBJECT DESIGN unfolds, the system definition is elaborated upon. As increasingly more detail is added, the implementation alternatives are decided. Each aspect (for example, attribute, operation, association, event, state) is considered. Operations are expanded into lower-level suboperations, and responsibility is assigned for each. Communications that were previously thought of simply as passed events (or data) are now mapped into specific implementation mechanisms. Following the frameworks and policies chosen during system design, the object designer adds implementation objects and optimizations, attempting to meet such project goals as efficiency, robustness, information hiding, and reuse.

DESIGNING SCENARIOS

MUCH OF THE work performed during the object design phase involves designing the details of the scenarios. We start with the output from analysis for a scenario of interest, and in order to get a better feel for the flow of control in this scenario, we construct the object message diagram that goes with the scenario.

CREATING OBJECT MESSAGE
DIAGRAMS IN RATIONAL ROSE

1. Choose Scenario Diagram from the Browse menu.
2. Double-click on < New > to display the New Scenario window.
3. Select the Object Message Diagram Type radio button.
4. Type the name of the scenario in the Title field of the New Scenario window.
5. Click the OK button.

CREATING OBJECTS AND MESSAGES IN
OBJECT MESSAGE DIAGRAMS IN RATIONAL ROSE

1. Click to select the object icon (rectangle) from the tool palette.
2. Click on the diagram window to draw the object.
3. Type the name of the object inside the rectangle.
4. Double-click on the object to display the Object Specification window.
5. Attach the object to a class by selecting the class name from the Class: pulldown menu.
6. Repeat the above steps for each object in the scenario.
7. To add a link for the message, select the link icon from the tool palette (solid line), click on the object sending the message, and drag the link to the receiving object.
8. To add the message arrow to the link, select the icon (arrow) from the tool palette and click on the link.
9. To create the message and make the message an operation of the receiving class, click the right mouse button on the message arrow.
10. Select either an existing operation or a new operation.
11. If you select a new operation, type the name of the operation in the Name field of the Operation Specification.
12. To make the newly created operation visible, click the right mouse button and select the operation from the list of operations.

The object message diagram for the "identify user" scenario follows on page 291.

ACTIVE OBJECTS

DURING ANALYSIS, MOST objects are considered to be active and independent, capable of initiating communications and responding to communications in any order, and in parallel. Now during design, realism must set in. Because active objects are more difficult to

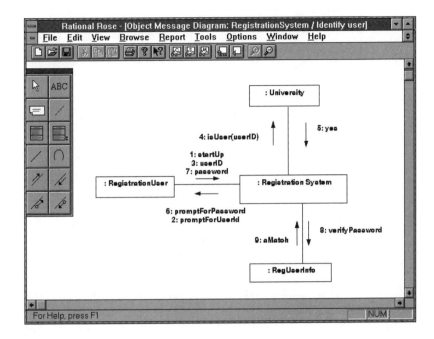

design and more costly in resources, some objects must be made passive and subordinate to others. Objects may be required to field requests from more than one active client, or an independent server may be created dynamically to handle each active client.

MAKING AN OBJECT ACTIVE IN RATIONAL ROSE

1. Select the object.
2. From the Browse menu, choose Referenced Item. This will bring up a class diagram that contains the class definition for this object.
3. Double-click on the class to bring up the Class Specification.
4. Select More . . .
5. From Concurrency, select the radio button that best describes the class's behavior. The Sequential button is used for normal software that assumes only one caller at a time; Guarded allows multiple callers if they properly behave themselves by calling appropriate guards; and

Active indicates that the class has its own thread of control. The Synchronous button allows multiple callers, and handles any required mutual exclusion internally.

MAPPING EVENTS

ANALYSIS DETERMINES ONLY the logical event flow among the domain and application objects; the mechanism for each of the event flows has not been specified. Now it is appropriate to determine how each event is to be transferred. In simple software systems, most events map to simple sequential operation calls or their returns. In these circumstances, control is passed along with the event on the operation call, and control is returned along with the event on the operation return. However, there are many ways of passing events, partially depending on the operating system and language technology, and partially depending on the design of the application structure.

The following list is a partial categorization of some of the more common ways of passing events in software.

- *Sequential operation call*—Control passes from the client to the server.

- *Sequential operation return*—Control returns to the client.

- *Asynchronous call*—One active object calls another, with control remaining in both.

- *Interrupt*—One active object interrupts another active object, causing the second's activity to be suspended or redirected, perhaps only temporarily.

- *Return from interrupt (RFI)*—An object returns to its normal activity after processing an interrupt.

- *Spawning*—The initiation of an independent thread of execution.

- *Termination*—The abandonment of an independent thread of execution.

- *Exception*—A thrown or raised exception or error condition that transfers control indirectly.

- *Resume*—The resumption of original processing after fielding a thrown condition.

- *Rendezvous*—A synchronizing call between independent threads of control.

- *Balking*—A call that is abandoned if the receiver is not ready for it.

- *Timed*—A call that is abandoned if no response is received within a specific time.

- *Message*—A tagged record being passed into a generic interface.

- *Polled*—The detection of a changed value when polling.

- *Queued*—An ordered, typically first-in, first-out (FIFO) posting of events.

- *Gates*—Flags (either logical or physical) set by one thread of control that allow or deny processing by another.

In practice, certain system-dependent combinations are primarily used in a given application.

IDENTIFYING EVENT MECHANISMS IN RATIONAL ROSE
1. If the event is being sent by a direct operation call, the message name has a trailing parenthesis (). Convert a message to an operation by selecting the event and bringing up the context-sensitive menu.
2. Create a new operation on the target class by selecting < New Operation >. Select OK when done.
3. Double click on the event and choose the operation from the Referenced Operation menu.
4. If the event (or operation) is sent by a timed, balking, synchronous, or asynchronous mechanism, double-click on the event and select the correct Synchronization radio button.

This will add a synchronization adornment to the flow arrow.

5. If a specific mechanism is being used, add descriptive text to the Documentation text box.

DATAFLOW DESIGN

WHEN DESIGNING SCENARIOS, it is necessary to determine how data flows among the objects. How will attributes be calculated? Where will operation parameters come from? How will the caller object see the destination object? The destination object may be seen across a standard association, or it may be seen because it is globally accessible, or it may be passed in as a parameter. The answers to these questions may reveal new operations, new attributes, and new links.

ADDING DATA FLOWS IN RATIONAL ROSE

1. Select the data item (the arrow with a circle for a tail) from the tool palette and place it on an existing message flow.

2. If the direction of the data flow is wrong, try again with the other data flow icon. It is possible to have more than one data flow flowing in both directions on a single message flow.

3. Type the name of the data item on the flow.

The following diagram on page 295 is an example of how the "start up" scenario may be designed. The details are for illustrative purposes only.

As we proceed, we update the object model and class definitions to contain the new objects, the new operations, and the new associations needed for the communications.

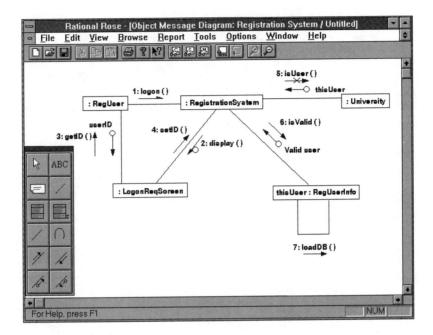

SUMMARY

DURING OBJECT DESIGN, we work through each scenario to find the flow of control during the scenario. We find map events to operations and other available techniques in an iterative manner to find lower and lower levels of operations. Find a target object for each operation identified, and identify the key data items being passed. Object interaction diagrams (based on the object message diagram) are constructed to indicate the flow of control and ordering of operations.

GLOSSARY

ACTIVE OBJECT

> An object that has its own thread of control and may execute independently of callers.

GUARDED OBJECT

An object that may be used by multiple active clients if the clients all cooperate.

SYNCHRONOUS OBJECT

An object that may be used by multiple active clients without the clients taking specific measures.

TARGET OBJECT

The object that an operation works on. Generally, the target object should be the object that is responsible for the operation.

Chapter 29

Design: Use of Commercial Class Libraries

PICKING A COMMERCIAL CLASS LIBRARY

THE FASTEST WAY to obtain reuse in any project is to buy the reuse-able elements. There are many commercial libraries on the market today for everything from GUI widgets and communication mechanisms to libraries geared toward certain vertical markets. Care must be taken when selecting the class libraries to be used in the project. Libraries should be evaluated using, at a minimum, the following criteria:

- *Completeness:* The library must provide a complete family of classes that provide all the capability the library claims to have.

- *Adaptability:* All platform-specific aspects must be clearly identified and isolated.

- *Efficiency:* Components must be easily assembled, must impose minimal run-time and memory overhead, and must be more reliable than hand-built mechanisms.

- *Simplicity:* The library must use a clear and consistent organization that makes it easy to identify and select appropriate classes.

- *Documentation:* Each class must be fully documented—developers would rather build their own class than reuse one that is hard to understand.

ADDING THE COMMERCIAL CLASSES TO THE MODEL

COMMERCIAL CLASS LIBRARIES can be reverse-engineered using the Rational Rose Analyzer. This tool reads C++ code and generates a .mdl file for Rational Rose. In the course registration problem, the Booch Components library was chosen as the foundation class library. Now is the time to incorporate the library into the registration model. By incorporating the library into the model under development, the designer can graphically show how the classes from analysis interact with the commercial classes.

SETTING UP A PROJECT IN THE
RATIONAL ROSE/C++ ANALYZER

1. Start the Rose/C++ Analyzer by double-clicking on the program icon.
2. Choose the New option from the File menu.
3. Click the caption button, type the name in the Caption window, and click the OK button.
4. Click the Directories button to display the Project Directory List window.
5. Select the desired directory and click the appropriate button: AddCurrent, Add Subdirs, or Add Hierarchy. Repeat this process until all directories have been added.
6. Click the OK button.
7. Click the Extensions button to display the Project File Extensions window.
8. Select the appropriate extensions and click the OK button.
9. Click the Files button to bring up the Project Files window.
10. To analyze all the files in the directory, click the Add All Files button.
11. To analyze only selected files, select the file and click the Add Files button.
12. Click the OK button.
13. The project is now set up. Choose the Save or the Save As option from the File menu to save the project.

The Analyzer window is shown in the following figure on page 301.

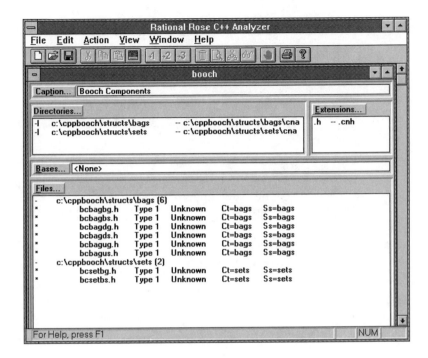

ANALYZING FILES WITH THE
RATIONAL ROSE/C++ ANALYZER

1. Click on the files to be analyzed.
2. Choose the Code Cycle option from the Actions menu. You will be asked if the files can be updated—click the Yes button. This inserts the markers that are needed by the code-generation capabilities of Rose.
3. When the analyzer is finished, the window is updated to show that the files have been code-cycled.

EXPORTING FILES FROM THE ROSE/C++ ANALYZER

1. Choose the Export Options option from the Edit menu.
2. Select the needed options.
3. Click the OK button.
4. Select the classes to be exported.
5. Choose the Export to Rose option from the Actions menu.

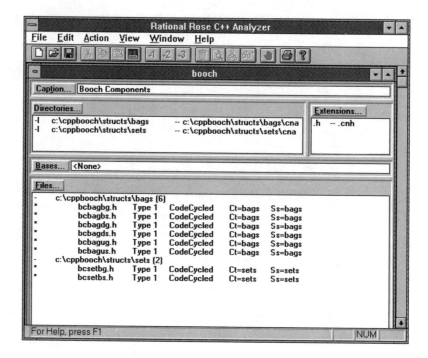

6. Click the OK button (or the Overwrite button if the model already exists).

Now that a model has been created by the analyzer, it can be viewed by loading the .mdl file into Rose.

VIEWING THE REVERSE-ENGINEERED MODEL IN RATIONAL ROSE

1. In Rose, choose Open from the File menu.
2. Select the .mdl file generated by the analyzer and click the OK button. The model contains categories for each directory. These categories should be recategorized as subcategories of the Booch Components category.
3. Select all the categories and choose the Cut option from the Edit menu to remove them from the diagram.
4. Create a new category called Booch Components.

5. Double-click on the Booch Components category to open it.
6. Choose the Paste option from the Edit menu to paste the previously cut categories.
7. With the categories still selected, choose the Relocate option from the Edit menu.

The diagrams are shown in the following figures.

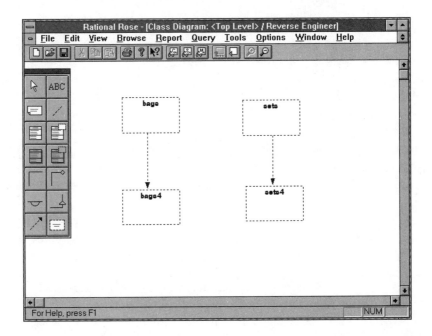

The next step involves making the Booch Components category a controlled unit. A .cat file will be created that can be loaded into other models.

MAKING CONTROLLED UNITS IN RATIONAL ROSE
1. Click on the category to be controlled to select it.
2. Choose the Units/Control option from the File menu.
3. Type the name of the .cat file in the File Name For Unit window.

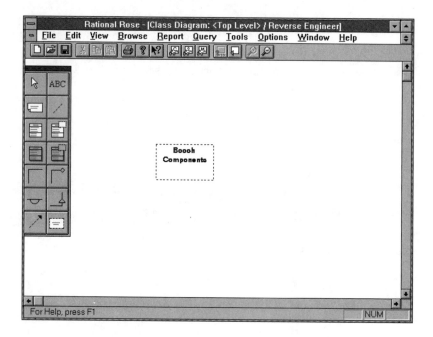

4. Click the OK button. The unit is created and marked with a U in an octagon.
5. The control unit adornment can be turned off by choosing the Display command from the Options menu.

The top-level class diagram follows on page 305.

The preceding process only has to be done once. The resulting .cat file is saved and can be loaded into any model.

LOADING CONTROL UNITS IN RATIONAL ROSE

1. Choose the Open option from the File menu.
2. Select the name of a .mdl file and click the OK button.
3. Select the Units/Load option from the File menu.
4. Select the .cat file to load.
5. Click the OK button.
    NOTE: If you have a place-holder category for the class library, Rose will ask if you want to overwrite the category. Click the Yes button to replace the category.

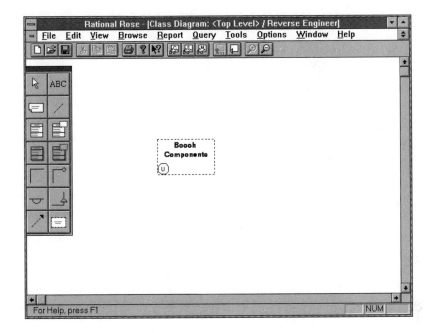

The top-level diagram for the course registration problem follows on page 306.

SUMMARY

THE FASTEST WAY to obtain reuse in any project is to buy it. Many commercial libraries are on the market today for everything from GUI Widgets and communication mechanisms to libraries geared toward certain vertical markets. Commercial class libraries can be reverse-engineered using the Rational Rose Analyzer. This tool reads C++ code and generates a .mdl file for Rational Rose. A category for the class library can be created, made into a controlled unit, and imported into the model for the current project. This provides the ability to show graphically how the classes from analysis interact with the commercial classes.

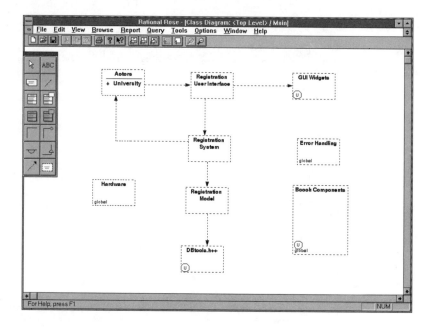

GLOSSARY

CLASS LIBRARY
> A collection of classes purchased from a vendor.

REVERSE-ENGINEER
> The ability to create a class diagram starting with existing code.

Chapter 30

Object Design: Designing Details

OBJECT DESIGN

NOW IS THE time to flesh out the architectural skeleton and follow the policies chosen during system design. The global design choices have been made; only local decisions are left unmade. Independent teams may now do the detailed design of the low-level components with a minimal amount of required cross-communication. They choose local solutions by employing familiar patterns, based on trading off the prioritized goals of efficiency, flexibility, robustness, and reuse, as well as cost and schedule. In the process, they may find it necessary to create additional entities that live behind the scenes in order to implement the design.

DESIGNING ATTRIBUTES

DESIGNING ATTRIBUTES IS generally straightforward. The obvious decision required concerns the internal representation of the attribute. Consider such properties as range and precision when choosing from the available primitive data types. In more complex circumstances, consider user-defined data types. If there are range constraints on the attributes, determine whether to enforce them and what design approaches to use for the constraints.

Consider encapsulating the implementation of the attribute from the using class. We do this when we feel uncertain about the optimal representation for the attribute, need to have enforced range constraints, or need to limit inappropriate operations on the attributes. In these circumstances, design the attribute type to be an abstract data type (ADT), and implement it with a class.

Determine the visibility of attributes. Typically, attributes are implemented as private, but they may have operations that can access them. Specify the access to these operations as private (–) if only the class has to have access, as protected (#) if the subclasses need access, or as public (+) if external access is needed.

In the ESU course registration problem, some of the attributes can be typed by commonly available types, such as char or int. The Booch Components library contains a string template class. A CharacterString class can be instantiated from the BC_TString

class and used as the implementation type for any attribute that is
a character string.

SPECIFYING ATTRIBUTE DETAILS IN RATIONAL ROSE

1. Double-click on the class to bring up the Class Specification
    sheet.
2. In the Attributes list box, double-click on the attribute to
    be specified to make the Attribute Specification window
    visible.
3. In the Type field, add the data type or class for the attribute.
4. Give an Initial Value to this attribute if a null value is not
    acceptable for this attribute when an object is created.
5. Set the Access for this attribute depending on the required
    visibility needed (attributes are typically private).
6. Set the Containment for this attribute to determine if the
    class will contain the attribute (By Value) or point to the
    attribute (by Reference).

The following figure shows the Attribute Specification for the
catalogSent attribute.

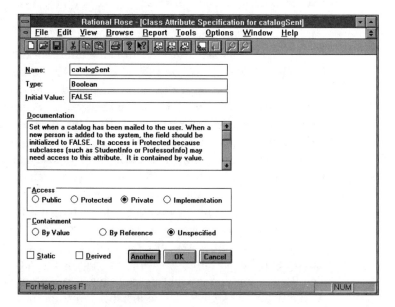

DESIGNING OPERATION PARAMETERS

IT IS ALSO necessary to specify the types of all the operation parameters and the types of any return values.

SPECIFYING ARGUMENT TYPES IN RATIONAL ROSE

1. Double-click on the class to bring up the Class Specification window.
2. In the Operations list box, double-click on the operation to make the Operation Specification window visible.
3. Double-click on an argument from the Arguments list box to make the Argument window visible.
4. Enter the name and type of the argument.
5. If this argument is optional, add the default value that will be used when the argument is not explicitly specified in the Default Value field.
6. Select the OK button, and repeat the above for each argument.
7. Enter the return type/class in the Return Class text box.

The following figure on page 312 shows the Operation Specification window for the verifyPassword operation.

DESIGNING ASSOCIATIONS

WE ALSO NEED to design each of the associations. During analysis, an association is considered to be binary; that is, it applies in both directions. However, during design only one direction may be needed. Starting at each object, determine if the association needs to be *navigable,* that is, if there is a need to traverse the association to the other role.

The multiplicity of each role needs to be reexamined for final specification. If the association is not navigable, then the multiplicity may be left unspecified.

As with attributes, we also need to decide the visibility and ownership of the association, that is, whether access to the target

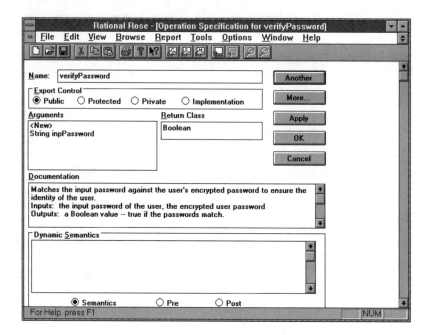

role is private, protected, or public, and whether the association is a containment or a reference. In the ESU course registration problem, the Password association will be implemented with one way pointers. Since the password may need to be available to the subclasses, they are protected.

SPECIFYING ASSOCIATION DETAILS IN RATIONAL ROSE

1. Double-click on the association to bring up the Association Specification window.
2. For each role, determine if the association needs to be traversed to that role. Have the Navigable flag set for that role if it must be traversed in that direction.
3. If navigable, consider adding the Role name to clarify meaning.
4. If navigable, specify the multiplicity in the Cardinality/Multiplicity box.
5. Set the Access for this association depending on the required visibility.

6. Set the Containment for this association to determine if the
    class will contain the attribute (By Value) or point to the
    attribute (by Reference).

The Association Specification follows.

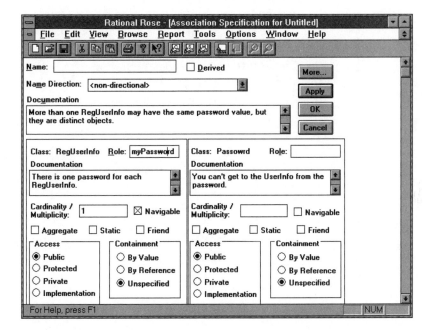

CONTAINER CLASSES

OFTEN WHERE THERE is a navigable *to-many* association, a container
class is needed to implement that direction. Container classes are
shown as parameterized classes in Rational Rose.

**CREATING PARAMETERIZED CLASS
INSTANTIATIONS IN RATIONAL ROSE**

1. Select the parameterized class icon (class with a dashed
    rectangle in the upper left corner) from the tool palette.
2. Click on the class diagram window.

3. Type the name of the class in the parameterized class icon.
4. Double-click on the class to bring up the Class Specification sheet. Select More . . .
5. Create parameters by clicking on < New > in the Formal Arguments list box. Enter the Name, Type, and Default Value.
6. Continue creating formal parameters until all parameters are made.
7. Create the instantiated class by using Create/Instantiated class from the Tools menu option.
8. Click on the class diagram window.
9. Type the name of the class in the instantiated class icon.
10. Double-click on the class to bring up the Class Specification sheet. Select More . . .
11. Create parameters by clicking on < New > in the Actual Arguments list box, and enter the Name.
12. Continue creating actual parameters until all parameters are made.
13. Select the instantiation relationship (dotted arrow) from the tool palette.
14. Drag the instantiation arrow from the instantiated class to the parameterized class.

A parameterized class is shown in the following class diagram on page 315.

CODE GENERATION

RATIONAL ROSE HAS a very powerful C++ code-generation capability. Options for the code generator are set using the Properties/Edit Properties option from the Tools menu. There are properties associated with the model, the class, relationships (association, uses, inherits), attributes, and operations. The properties applying to the model as a whole involve file names, default container names, and the placement of the generated code. Class properties involve the generation of constructors, destructors, copy constructors, equality operators, and get/set methods. The property set for relationships and attributes

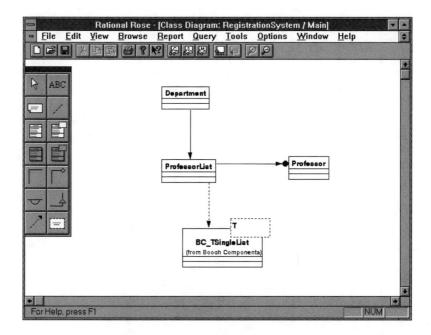

deals with the construction of get/set methods, visibility of the methods, and the container class to be used. Operation properties deal with the operation kind (common, virtual, abstract, static, or friend) and allow the operation to be made constant.

These property sets may be edited, and new sets may be created to specify the C++ features needed for the project. Two files are generated for each class: a header (.h) file and an implementation (.cpp) file.

GENERATING CODE IN RATIONAL ROSE

1. Click on a class or category.
2. Edit the property sets or create new property sets if needed by clicking on the appropriate element (class, relationship, attribute, or operation) and selecting the Properties/Edit Properties option from the Tools menu.
3. Choose the Generate C++ Code option from the Tools menu. Code is generated, and all messages are written to the log.

Appendix C presents the code generated for the Course class (using the default property sets).

The final step of the process is to add the method code to the preserved regions in the .cpp file and test the classes. Each class should be tested by itself to see that it does what it is supposed to do, and as a class participating in a scenario to be sure that all collaborations are correct.

SUMMARY

DURING OBJECT DESIGN, the details of all the model components are determined. As individual scenarios are explored, operations and attributes are identified and specified, and additional opportunities for reuse are identified.

GLOSSARY

ABSTRACT DATA TYPES (ADT)

A strongly typed attribute type. The internal representation of an ADT is encapsulated from the outside. ADTs are used to hide implementation details, to enforce range constraints, to limit otherwise available operations, and to set initial values.

INSTANTIATED CLASS

A class that is made from a parameterized class by using specific values for the parameters.

NAVIGABLE

The quality that allows an association to be traversed from one side to the other.

PARAMETERIZED CLASS

A class that serves as a template, or blueprint, for other classes that may be tailored by supplying values for parameters.

Chapter 31

Evolution: Building the Next Release

■

Using Reverse-Engineering to Set the
Stage for the Next Architectural Release

■

Summary

■

Glossary

USING REVERSE-ENGINEERING TO SET THE STAGE FOR THE NEXT ARCHITECTURAL RELEASE

THE MODEL MUST be updated to reflect any design-level changes made to the code (e.g., helping methods added, new classes added) while implementing the current release. Rather than updating the model by hand, we can use the reverse-engineering capability of Rose to generate a model based on the current implementation, and this information can be merged into the design model.

REVERSE ENGINEERING USING THE ROSE/C++ ANALYZER

1. Set up a Rose/C++ project; remember to include all directories referenced by your code. Tip: Set up a base project for the C++ libraries and any class library used.
2. Select the files to be analyzed.
3. Choose the Code Cycle option from the Actions menu.
4. Export the code to Rose, making sure you export to a *new* model name. *Do not overwrite* your design model.

The course registration problem uses the Booch Components class library. The project booch.pjt was created to reverse-engineer this library, and it can be used as a base project here.

The following figure on page 320 shows the Analyzer window.

Once the files are analyzed, the information is exported to Rose. The name of the model created is course.mdl.

This information must now be imported into the design model.

UPDATING MODELS IN RATIONAL ROSE

1. Choose the Open option from the File menu.
2. Choose the original design model and click the OK button.
3. Choose the Update option from the File menu.

4. Enter the name of the reverse-engineered model just created
   by the analyzer in the File Name field on the Update Model
   From window.

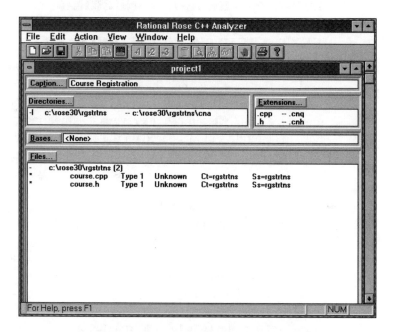

SUMMARY

THE MODEL MUST be updated to reflect any changes made while implementing the previous release. Rather than updating the model by hand, we use the reverse-engineering capability of Rose to generate a model based on the current implementation. Then we import this information to update the design model.

GLOSSARY

BASE PROJECT
> A project that supplements the information in a program-specific project, usually with information about header files for compiler-specific libraries or other class libraries being used.

DESIGN MODEL
> A model that reflects the current design of the problem at hand.

Chapter 32

Evolution: Team Development with Rational Rose

PARALLEL DEVELOPMENT AND CLASS CATEGORIES

FOR THE MAJORITY of systems, a large number of classes are developed very quickly. The most effective way to subdivide the system is to use the concept of the class category (and its subcategories) as a unit of work. Breaking up the model into individual units allows it to be simultaneously manipulated by different teams of analysts, architects, and developers. Good practice dictates that a unit should be owned by one person. Since a category can be made up of nested categories, this strategy can be applied to the Rose model under creation.

Each category is an individual control unit, and the model is the sum of all the categories contained in it. Persistence is achieved by placing each unit in an individual file (.cat file). We have already seen how to create a control unit in Rose (Chapter 12); each category should be created as its own unit. The top-level diagram for the registration problem follows.

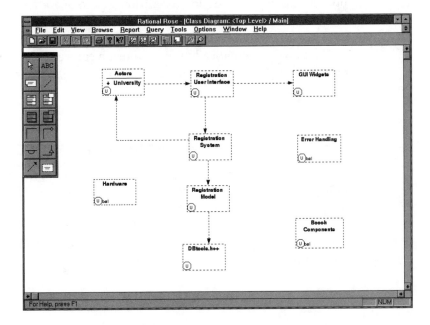

The adornment (symbol) for a control unit is a *U* in an octagon. This can be turned off by choosing the Display/Unit Adornments command from the Options menu.

Because each category is a separate unit, the whole model does not have to be loaded when we open the model. This allows a large model to be opened quickly. On opening a model, the user is asked if the subunits should be loaded. If the answer is no, then the unit will not be loaded until needed (when the category is opened by double-clicking on it).

Each unit in the model can also be write-protected. This allows a user to view the classes in the category but not to change them.

WRITE-PROTECTING CATEGORIES IN RATIONAL ROSE
1. Click on the category to be write-protected.
2. Choose the Units/Write Protect < category name > option from the File menu.

When the write-protected category is opened, toolbars are not displayed on any of the diagrams. Furthermore, when a class is opened, the < New > option for attributes and operations is not available. Thus, an analyst or designer may view the classes in the category but not change the category.

Rose will automatically write-protect a control unit if the unit's access control in the platform file system is specified as read-only.

INTEGRATION WITH CONFIGURATION-MANAGEMENT SYSTEMS

IN ORDER TO facilitate true multiuser management of the model units, each category file is placed under configuration-management (CM) control. Rose menu selections may be customized to add CM menu selections such as Check In, Check Out, Accept Changes, and Control. This is accomplished by creating a menu specification file, which Rose reads at startup.

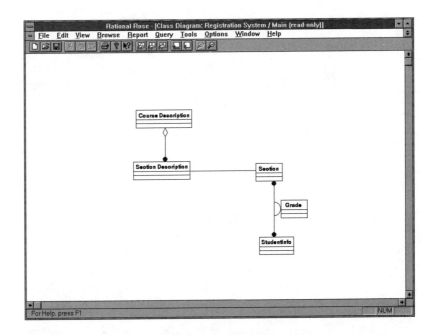

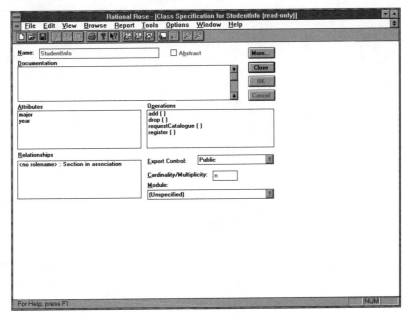

SUMMARY

SIMULTANEOUS MANIPULATION OF a model by teams of analysts, architects, and developers can be achieved by separating a model into individual control units. The ability to control individual units, coupled with Rose's ability to integrate with commercial configuration-management systems, enables team members to synchronize parallel activities and maintain multiple versions of its controlled units.

GLOSSARY

CONTROL UNIT

> A unit, such as a category or subsystem, that can be loaded or saved independently and integrated into a configuration-management system.

Booch Notation

■

Class Diagrams

■

Object Message Diagrams

■

Message Trace Diagrams

■

State Transition Diagrams

■

Module Diagrams

■

Process Diagrams

CLASS DIAGRAMS

CLASS DIAGRAMS DEPICT the static view of the system. They show the existence of classes and their relationships in the logical design of a system. A class diagram may represent all or part of the class structure of a system.

Class Icons

Class Category
A category is a logical collection of classes. The classes in a class category collaborate to provide a set of services.

Catagory Name

Class
A class is a set of objects that share a common structure and common behavior.

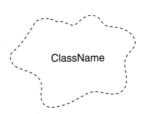

Class Utility

A class utility is a collection of free subprograms or, in C++, a class that only provides static members and/or static member functions.

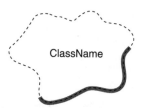

Parameterized Class

A parameterized class is a class that serves as a template for other classes, in which the template may be parameterized by other classes, objects, and operations.

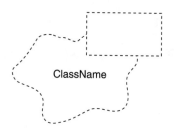

Instantiated Class

A parameterized class must be instantiated (its parameters filled in) before instances can be created.

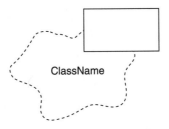

Metaclass

A metaclass is a class whose instances are themselves classes.

Class Relationships

Association

An association is a bidirectional semantic connection between two classes.

"Has" Relationship

A "has" relationship is a stronger form of association in which the relationship is between the whole and its parts.

"Uses" Relationship

A "uses" relationship denotes a client/supplier relationship in which the client depends upon the supplier to provide certain services, but the client does not contain semantic knowledge about the supplier.

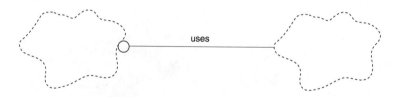

Role Names

Role names can be created to add clarity to the model.

Attributed Association
An attributed association involves structure and behavior belonging
to the relationship as opposed to the classes in the relationship.

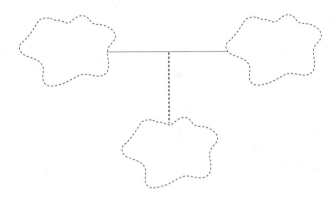

Inheritance
Inheritance is a relationship between a superclass and its subclasses.

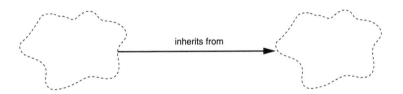

Containment Adornments

Containment by Value
Containment by value implies that one object physically contains
another object. The lifetimes of the two objects in the relationship
are connected.

Containment by Reference

Containment by reference implies that one object contains a pointer, or reference, to another object. The two objects in the relationship have independent lifetimes.

Class Properties

Abstract

An abstract class is one that does not have any instances.

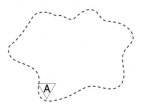

Static

The static adornment is used to show that the source class owns the target class. In C++ this translates to a static data member, and in Smalltalk this translates to a class variable.

Friend

The friendship adornment is used to show that the target class has granted access to its private parts to the source class.

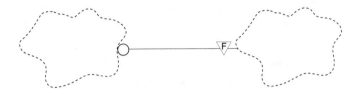

Virtual

The virtual adornment is used to show virtual inheritance (one copy of a common base class).

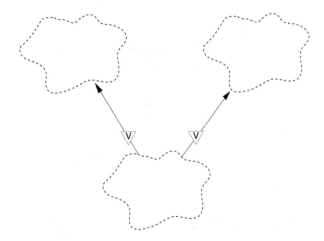

Export Control

Public

A public declaration forms part of the interface of a class, object, or module, and is visible to all other classes, objects, and modules that have visibility to it.

Protected |

A protected declaration forms part of the interface of a class, object, or module, but it is not visible to any other classes, objects, or modules except those that represent subclasses.

Private ||

A private declaration forms part of the interface of a class, object, or module, but it is not visible to any other classes, objects, or modules.

Notes

A note is a textual description of assumptions and decisions that may be attached to the model.

OBJECT MESSAGE DIAGRAMS

OBJECT MESSAGE DIAGRAMS show the existence of objects and their relationships in the logical design of a system. An object message diagram may represent all or part of the object structure of a system, and it primarily illustrates the semantics of mechanisms in the logical design. A single object message diagram represents a snapshot in time.

Object

An object is something you can do things to. Each object has state, behavior, and identity, and is a member of a class.

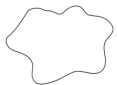

Link

A link is an instance of an association. It is a pathway for communication between objects.

Message

A message identifies some work that one object performs upon another in order to elicit a reaction.

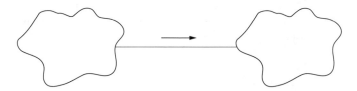

Simple Synchronization

A message between two objects in the same thread of control involves simple synchronization. The client object waits for the supplier object to complete the invoked operation.

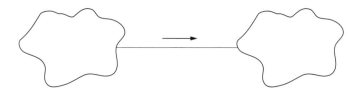

Synchronous Synchronization

A message between two objects in different threads of control. The client object broadcasts the message and passively waits for an indefinite time for acknowledgment from the supplier object.

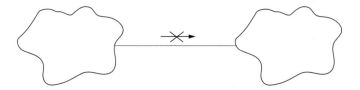

Timeout

A message between two objects in different threads of control that involves a timeout. The client object broadcasts the message and waits a certain amount of time for acknowledgment from the supplier object.

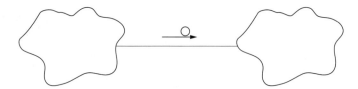

Balking Synchronization

Balking synchronization characterizes a message between two objects in different threads of control. The client object broadcasts the message and waits for a time of zero for acknowledgment from the supplier object; thus, the supplier must be waiting for the message.

Asynchronous Synchronization

A message between two objects in different threads of control that involves asynchronous synchronization. The client object broadcasts the message and resumes operation without waiting for acknowledgment from the supplier object.

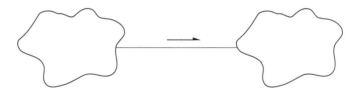

MESSAGE TRACE DIAGRAMS

MESSAGE TRACE DIAGRAMS show the existence of objects and their relationships in the logical design of a system. A message trace diagram may represent all or part of the object structure of a system, and primarily illustrates the semantics of mechanisms in the logical design. A single object diagram represents a snapshot in time. A message trace diagram is an alternate way of representing the information on an object diagram.

Object

An object is something you can do things to. Each object has state, behavior, and identity, and is a member of a class.

Event

An event is some occurrence that may cause the state of a system to change.

Operation

An operation is some work that one object performs upon another in order to elicit a reaction.

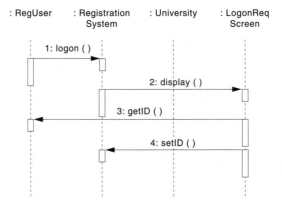

STATE TRANSITION DIAGRAMS

STATE TRANSITION DIAGRAMS show the state space of a given class, the events that cause a transition from one state to another, and the actions that result from a state change.

State

State is one of the possible conditions in which an object may exist.

Start State

The state of an object upon creation is its start state.

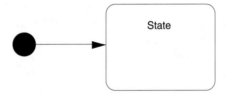

Stop State

The state of an object before destruction is its stop state.

State transitions

State transitions involve the passing of an object from one state to another.

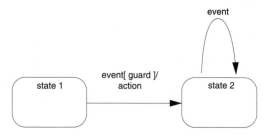

Entry/Exit Actions and Activities

An entry action is an action performed upon entering a state.
An exit action is an an action performed before leaving a state.
An activity is an operation that occurs while in a state.

State
entry: action do: activity exit: action

Superstate

A superstate provides the ability to nest states in a state transition diagram.

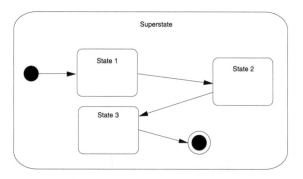

MODULE DIAGRAMS

MODULE DIAGRAMS SHOW the allocation of classes and objects to modules in the physical design of a system. A module diagram may represent all or part of the module architecture of a system.

Main Program
A main program represents a file that contains the root of a program.

Specification
A specification represents a file that contains the declaration of a class.

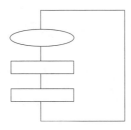

Body

A body represents a file that contains the implementation of a class.

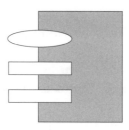

Subsystem

Subsystems serve to partition the physical model of a system. A subsystem is an aggregate containing other modules, and it may contain other subsystems.

PROCESS DIAGRAMS

PROCESS DIAGRAMS SHOW the allocation of processes to processors in the physical design of a system. A process diagram may represent all or part of the process architecture of a system.

Processor

A processor is a piece of hardware that has computational resources.

Device

A device is a piece of hardware that does not have computational resources.

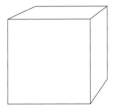

Connection

A connection represents some type of hardware coupling between two entities, where an entity is either a processor or a device.

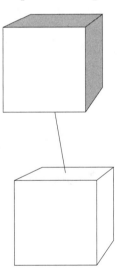

Appendix B

OMT Notation

- Object Model

- Dynamic Model

- Functional Model

OBJECT MODEL

THE OBJECT MODEL depicts the static view of the system. It shows the existence of classes and their relationships in the logical design of a system.

Class Icons

Class Category

A category is a logical collection of classes. The classes in a class category collaborate to provide a set of services.

```
┌ ─ ─ ─ ─ ─ ─ ─ ┐
│   Category    │
│     Name      │
│               │
└ ─ ─ ─ ─ ─ ─ ─ ┘
```

Class

A class is a set of objects that share a common structure and common behavior.

```
┌─────────────┐
│  ClassName  │
├─────────────┤
├─────────────┤
└─────────────┘
```

Class Utility

A class utility is a collection of free subprograms or, in C++, a class that only provides static members and/or static member functions.

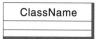

Parameterized Class

A parameterized class is a class that serves as a template for other classes, in which the template may be parameterized by other classes, objects, and/or operations.

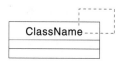

Class Relationships

Association

An association is a bidirectional semantic connection between two classes.

Aggregation

An aggregation is a stronger form of association in which the relationship is between the whole and its parts.

Role Names

Role names can be added to associations in order to add clarity to the model.

Link Attribute

A link attribute involves structure and behavior belonging to the relationship itself as opposed to the classes in the relationship.

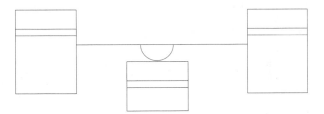

Inheritance

Inheritance is a relationship between a superclass and its subclasses.

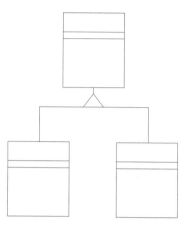

Multiplicity

Exactly one

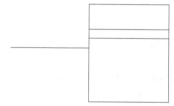

Many (zero or more)

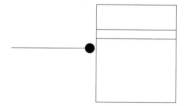

One or more

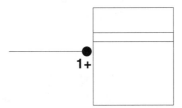

Optional (zero or one)

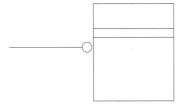

Numerically specified

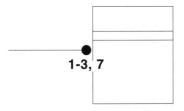

Export Control

Public   +
A public declaration forms part of the interface of a class, object, or module, and is visible to all other classes, objects, and modules that have visibility to it.

Protected   #
A protected declaration forms part of the interface of a class, object, or module, but is not visible to any other classes, objects, or modules except those that represent subclasses.

Private   —

A private declaration forms part of the interface of a class, object, or module, but is not visible to any other classes, objects, or modules.

DYNAMIC MODEL

THE DYNAMIC MODEL shows the existence of objects and their relationships in the logical design of a system. State transition diagrams show the state space of a given class, the events that cause a transition from one state to another, and the actions that result from a state change.

State

State is one of the possible conditions in which an object may exist.

Start State

The state of an object upon creation is its start state.

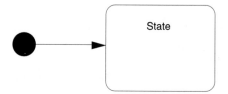

Stop State

The state of an object before destruction is its stop state.

State transitions

State transitions involve the passing of an object from one state to another.

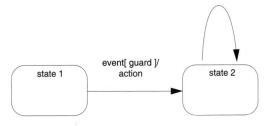

Entry/Exit Actions and Activities

An entry action is an action performed upon entering a state.
An exit action is an action performed before leaving a state.
An activity is an operation that occurs while in a state.

Superstate

Superstates provide the ability to nest states in a state transition diagram.

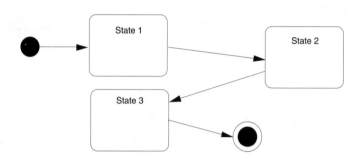

The Message Trace Diagram

Message trace diagrams show the existence of objects and their relationships in the logical design of a system. A message trace diagram may represent all or part of the object structure of a system, and primarily illustrates the semantics of mechanisms in the logical design. A single object diagram represents a snapshot in time.

Object

An object is something you can do things to. Each object has state, behavior, and identity, and is a member of a class.

Event

An event is some occurrence that may cause the state of a system to change.

Operation

An operation is some work that one object performs upon another in order to elicit a reaction.

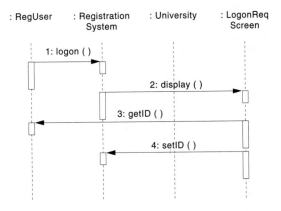

FUNCTIONAL MODEL

THE FUNCTIONAL MODEL shows the interaction between objects in the system.

Object

An object is something you can do things to. Each object has state, behavior, and identity, and is a member of a class.

Link

A link is an instance of an association. It is a pathway for communication between objects.

Message

A message identifies some work that one object performs upon another in order to elicit a reaction.

Dataflow

A data return may be used to show the flow of data across a link between two objects.

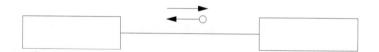

Appendix C

Sample Code
Generated by Rational Rose

Course.h

```
//## begin module.cm preserve=no
//         %X% %Q% %Z% %W%
//## end module.cm

//## begin module.cp preserve=no
//## end module.cp

//## Module: Course; Pseudo Package specification
//## Subsystem: RegistrationSystem
//## Source file: c:\rose30\rgstrtns\course.h

#ifndef Course_h
#define Course_h 1

//## begin module.additionalIncludes preserve=no
//## end module.additionalIncludes

//## begin module.includes preserve=yes
//## end module.includes

//## begin module.additionalDeclarations preserve=yes
//## end module.additionalDeclarations

//## Class: Course
//## Category: RegistrationSystem
//## Subsystem: RegistrationSystem
//## Persistence: Transient
//## Cardinality/Multiplicity: n

class Course
{
//## begin Course.initialDeclarations preserve=yes
//## end Course.initialDeclarations

public:
//## Constructors (generated)
Course();

Course(const Course &right);

//## Destructor (generated)
~Course();

//## Assignment Operation (generated)
const Course & operator=(const Course &right);

//## Equality Operations (generated)
int operator==(const Course &right) const;
```

```
        int operator!=(const Course &right) const;


        //## Other Operations (specified)
        //## Operation: addStudent%817515258
        void addStudent(Student& newStudent);

        //## Operation: courseAvailable%817515259
        Boolean courseAvailable();

        //## Operation: create%817515260
        void create();

        //## Operation: save%817515261
        void save();

        // Additional Public Declarations
        //## begin Course.public preserve=yes
        //## end Course.public

    protected:
        // Additional Protected Declarations
        //## begin Course.protected preserve=yes
        //## end Course.protected

    private:
        //## Get and Set Operations for Class Attributes (generated)

        //## Attribute: description
        const CharacterString get_description() const;
        void set_description(const CharacterString value);

        //## Attribute: daysOffered
        const CharacterString get_daysOffered() const;
        void set_daysOffered(const CharacterString value);

        //## Attribute: startTime
        const BC_TString get_startTime() const;
        void set_startTime(const BC_TString value);

        //## Attribute: endTime
        const BC_TString get_endTime() const;
        void set_endTime(const BC_TString value);

        //## Attribute: location
        const CharacterString get_location() const;
        void set_location(const CharacterString value);

        //## Attribute: section
        const CharacterString get_section() const;
```

```
void set_section(const CharacterString value);

//## Attribute: title
const CharacterString get_title() const;
void set_title(const CharacterString value);

// Additional Private Declarations
//## begin Course.private preserve=yes
//## end Course.private

private:  //## implementation
// Data Members for Class Attributes

//## begin Course::description.attr preserve=no  Private:
    CharacterString {U}
CharacterString description;
//## end Course::description.attr

//## begin Course::daysOffered.attr preserve=no  Private:
    CharacterString {U}
CharacterString daysOffered;
//## end Course::daysOffered.attr

//## begin Course::startTime.attr preserve=no  Private:
    BC_TString {U}
BC_TString startTime;
//## end Course::startTime.attr

//## begin Course::endTime.attr preserve=no  Private:
    BC_TString {U}
BC_TString endTime;
//## end Course::endTime.attr

//## begin Course::location.attr preserve=no  Private:
    CharacterString {U}
CharacterString location;
//## end Course::location.attr

//## begin Course::section.attr preserve=no  Private:
    CharacterString {U}
CharacterString section;
//## end Course::section.attr

//## begin Course::title.attr preserve=no  Private:
    CharacterString {U}
CharacterString title;
//## end Course::title.attr

// Additional Implementation Declarations
//## begin Course.implementation preserve=yes
```

```
//## end Course.implementation

};

// Class Course

//## Get and Set Operations for Class Attributes (inline)

inline const CharacterString Course::get_description() const
{
//## begin Course::get_description%.get preserve=no
return description;
//## end Course::get_description%.get
}

inline void Course::set_description(const CharacterString value)
{
//## begin Course::set_description%.set preserve=no
description=value;
//## end Course::set_description%.set
}

inline const CharacterString Course::get_daysOffered() const
{
//## begin Course::get_daysOffered%.get preserve=no
return daysOffered;
//## end Course::get_daysOffered%.get
}

inline void Course::set_daysOffered(const CharacterString value)
{
//## begin Course::set_daysOffered%.set preserve=no
daysOffered=value;
//## end Course::set_daysOffered%.set
}

inline const BC_TString Course::get_startTime() const
{
//## begin Course::get_startTime%.get preserve=no
return startTime;
//## end Course::get_startTime%.get
}

inline void Course::set_startTime(const BC_TString value)
{
//## begin Course::set_startTime%.set preserve=no
startTime=value;
//## end Course::set_startTime%.set
}
```

```
inline const BC_TString Course::get_endTime() const
{
//## begin Course::get_endTime%.get preserve=no
return endTime;
//## end Course::get_endTime%.get
}

inline void Course::set_endTime(const BC_TString value)
{
//## begin Course::set_endTime%.set preserve=no
endTime=value;
//## end Course::set_endTime%.set
}

inline const CharacterString Course::get_location() const
{
//## begin Course::get_location%.get preserve=no
return location;
//## end Course::get_location%.get
}

inline void Course::set_location(const CharacterString value)
{
//## begin Course::set_location%.set preserve=no
location=value;
//## end Course::set_location%.set
}

inline const CharacterString Course::get_section() const
{
//## begin Course::get_section%.get preserve=no
return section;
//## end Course::get_section%.get
}

inline void Course::set_section(const CharacterString value)
{
//## begin Course::set_section%.set preserve=no
section=value;
//## end Course::set_section%.set
}

inline const CharacterString Course::get_title() const
{
//## begin Course::get_title%.get preserve=no
return title;
//## end Course::get_title%.get
}

inline void Course::set_title(const CharacterString value)
```

```
        {
        //## begin Course::set_title%.set preserve=no
        title=value;
        //## end Course::set_title%.set
        }

        #endif
```

Course.cpp

```
        //## begin module.cm preserve=no
        //          %X% %Q% %Z% %W%
        //## end module.cm

        //## begin module.cp preserve=no
        //## end module.cp

        //## Module: Course; Pseudo Package body
        //## Subsystem: RegistrationSystem
        //## Source file: c:\rose30\rgstrtns\course.cpp


        //## begin module.additionalIncludes preserve=no
        //## end module.additionalIncludes

        //## begin module.includes preserve=yes
        //## end module.includes

        // Course
        #include "RgstrtnS\Course.h"

        //## begin module.additionalDeclarations preserve=yes
        //## end module.additionalDeclarations


        // Class Course

        Course::Course()
        //## begin Course::Course%.hasinit preserve=no
        //## end Course::Course%.hasinit
        //## begin Course::Course%.initialization preserve=yes
        //## end Course::Course%.initialization
        {
        //## begin Course::Course%.body preserve=yes
        //## end Course::Course%.body
        }

        Course::Course(const Course &right)
        //## begin Course::Course%copy.hasinit preserve=no
        //## end Course::Course%copy.hasinit
```

```
//## begin Course::Course%copy.initialization preserve=yes
//## end Course::Course%copy.initialization
{
//## begin Course::Course%copy.body preserve=yes
//## end Course::Course%copy.body
}


Course::~Course()
{
//## begin Course::~Course%.body preserve=yes
//## end Course::~Course%.body
}


const Course & Course::operator=(const Course &right)
{
//## begin Course::operator=%.body preserve=yes
//## end Course::operator=%.body
}


int Course::operator==(const Course &right) const
{
//## begin Course::operator==%.body preserve=yes
//## end Course::operator==%.body
}

int Course::operator!=(const Course &right) const
{
//## begin Course::operator!=%.body preserve=yes
//## end Course::operator!=%.body
}


//## Other Operations (implementation)
void Course::addStudent(Student& newStudent)
{
//## begin Course::addStudent%817515258.body preserve=yes
//## end Course::addStudent%817515258.body
}

Boolean Course::courseAvailable()
{
//## begin Course::courseAvailable%817515259.body
   preserve=yes
//## end Course::courseAvailable%817515259.body
}
```

```
void Course::create()
{
//## begin Course::create%817515260.body preserve=yes
//## end Course::create%817515260.body
}

void Course::save()
{
//## begin Course::save%817515261.body preserve=yes
//## end Course::save%817515261.body
}


// Additional Declarations
//## begin Course.declarations preserve=yes
//## end Course.declarations
```

Index